PONDS AND LAKES FOR WILDFOWL

PONDS AND LAKES FOR WILDFOWL

Illustrations by Malcolm Kaye

Published by
THE GAME CONSERVANCY
Fordingbridge
Hampshire SP6 1EF
Telephone No : 0425 652381

ISBN 0 9500130 4 8

All photographs, unless otherwise stated,
by Game Conservancy Ltd.

Printed and bound in Great Britain by
BAS Printers Limited, Over Wallop, Hampshire

Published by
Game Conservancy Ltd
Fordingbridge, Hampshire SP6 1EF

CONTENTS

CHAPTER ONE

Introduction – Wetlands and the Conservation of Wildfowl

A map of the British Isles shows that only a tiny proportion of the land surface is occupied by freshwater wetlands, yet these areas support an unusually rich, diverse and unique plant and animal community, making up a disproportionately large part of our national wildlife heritage. They are, therefore, an important asset in terms of the conservation of wetland species.

The European populations of waterfowl are obviously a major part of this wetland community, and these and many other wetland bird species are largely migratory, having no regard for national frontiers. They form an international wildlife resource, with an enormous cultural, aesthetic, scientific and sporting value and, as such, demand measures to conserve them and their habitats.

The purpose of wildfowl conservation, as defined by the Wildfowl Conservation Committee of the then Nature Conservancy Council in 1960, is: "To safeguard the species of wildfowl and to maintain existing stocks in at least their present strengths and their present distribution". The role of wildfowl refuges is "to safeguard species with a limited distribution in this country, to act as wildfowl strongholds, form wildfowl reservoirs and provide centres from which less common species can be encouraged to increase their range".

A very large number of European waterfowl winter in Britain and so the survival of the many species of wildfowl, wader and other birds which breed in the far north depends to a large degree upon the existence of food and shelter provided in the wetlands of Britain, either on their migration south or throughout the winter. We therefore have a responsibility to provide and maintain sufficient wetland habitat for them.

Our own resident water and waterside birds rely on these habitats the whole year through and we are host to a great number of visiting breeding species of wetland birds in summer. It is important that our wetlands should be capable of supporting productive breeding populations to enable these residents and visitors to maintain their numbers.

It is clear that the disappearance of wetlands in this country has a detrimental effect on a major wildlife resource of international importance.

It is an unfortunate fact that the greater part of Britain's natural wetlands have now gone and many of those remaining are still under threat. Inland and estuarine fens and marshes are either drained, or filled in and reclaimed, ponds and lakes are polluted, degraded or simply over used for recreation, rivers are canalised and surface water is rushed away to sea by improvements in land drainage.

Despite the large scale and continuing reduction in area of natural wetland habitats, and with present levels of degradation due to pollution and increasing recreational use, most of our wild waterfowl are currently holding their own, but are still under pressure. In this situation their conservation can be aided by relatively small scale activities carried out at a local level, largely because of the ability of waterfowl to exploit new habitats successfully.

The role of new ponds and lakes

Against this background, any new water body can have a great potential role to play in achieving the aims of conservation of wetland species, and man-made wetlands such as water storage and river regulation reservoirs, clay pits, peat diggings, farm ponds, lakes and gravel pits assume an increasing importance for the conservation of wetland communities. As more than 80% of the land surface of Britain is farmed, it is clear that the welfare of much of our wetland wildlife depends upon positive action by farmers to retain and create a range of such habitats.

Reservoirs sometimes suffer from the disadvantages of great depth and widely fluctuating water levels and clay pits are usually

2

too deep to be of any great value in a biologically productive sense, although both have great value as winter roosts for waterfowl if they are not disturbed. Wet lowland peat workings, like those of the Somerset Levels, are a special case and while they do require very careful and sensitive restoration and management to retain the unique character of peatlands, this is outside the scope of this book. Such restoration can take many decades; for example the Norfolk Broads, which now enjoy SSSI status, were originally peat diggings in the Middle Ages. Of all the man-made "new wetlands", farm ponds, lakes and gravel pits lend themselves most readily to the creation of the ideal conditions necessary to meet the needs of both resident and migrant, breeding and wintering wildfowl.

In the current climate of reducing surplus agricultural production, more opportunities are arising for farmers to create new conservation habitats. The construction of a wetland (pond or lake, with some surrounding wet marsh) on a farm is without doubt one of the most cost effective ways of increasing the overall richness and variety of wildlife species on the farm. Both good management of an existing wetland and the creation of a new well planned one make real contributions to the conservation of those species which depend upon such habitats.

Large bodies of open water which provide the necessary winter roosts, safeguarding the welfare of the birds over the winter so that there are sufficient survivors in good condition, able to re-populate their northern breeding grounds, are now fairly common, particularly in the south-east. What is required more urgently is well managed waterfowl production areas which our resident breeding waterbirds can use successfully to maintain their populations at a healthy level. The creation and subsequent management of ponds and lakes as habitat for breeding birds is thus the most important aspect of wildfowl conservation.

A secluded, well screened farm pond or lake, which contains all of the desirable features, ie a range of depths but mainly shallows; a rich variety of water plants, from marginal reeds and floating leaved forms down to deeper, submerged species; a number of islands; gently sloping shores, some of them open, mown, gravelled or grazed; the whole surrounded by good tall meadow nesting cover and sheltered by a tree belt and/or hedge and stockproof fence, will be real haven for a whole range of wildlife.

In addition to attracting ducks, geese, swans, coots, moorhens, grebes, etc., it will create homes for a vast array of water animals including some spectacular dragonflies and many frogs, newts and toads. It will contain lots of water plants which are themselves worth conserving, and the surrounding piece of wilderness will support many species of butterflies, moths, other insects and a multitude of waterside and farmland birds (including game) and small mammals. It will become a real oasis of wildlife and an asset as a highly attractive landscape feature. In addition, a pond or lake provides a valuable sporting asset, is useful for stock watering, crop irrigation and, if relatively close to the farm buildings, as an emergency source of water in case of fire.

The aims of this book

This book is concerned primarily with the development of good habitats for wildfowl. It also covers areas of management which, although they are of some benefit to wildfowl, are possibly of greater value to other wildlife groups. For example, the sound management of coppice and scrub is good for some nesting ducks, but it is of far greater value in maintaining habitat for warblers and insects; similarly, meadow management may be aimed at providing tall, dense ground cover for nesting wildfowl, but those meadows are probably of greater conservation value for botanical and entomological reasons.

It will be seen that wetlands require a degree of management to maintain the optimum conditions for wildlife. In many ways the existence of a healthy, productive population of breeding waterfowl is an indicator or "barometer" of good conditions within a wetland and the wider conservation value of wetlands managed for wildfowl production and sporting use is very considerable.

In considering the creation of a pond or lake on any area of farmland one should first decide the aims of the exercise – what is it required for – fishing, shooting, a landscape feature, or general conservation? Having established the objectives, can they be met by improvement to or better management of an existing wetland, or is it desirable to create a new one?

Either way, one can then, in the light of the information contained within this book, identify and examine each and every possible site to evaluate its potential to produce a water body which will satisfy the original aims.

The various sections of the book should then guide you through the steps in the creation of the new habitats, and show you how to manage the site to the best effect. We have tried to answer in sequence such questions as: what makes a good pond or lake for wildfowl, how big does it need to be, how deep, what shape, and what type of habitats must it contain to ensure that it meets the needs of wildfowl? With what plant species, when and how should it be planted? Can what is proposed in the way of a pond or lake be done legally? Is there any chance of grant aid?

Where should it be sited and what method of construction can be used? How should an earth dam be made? Can good habitats be made by the restoration of a gravel pit; if so, how? When it is established and colonised, when, how and why must it be managed? Finally we describe how to stock a pond or lake with mallard and examine the sporting use for fishing and shooting, which often provide the economic justification for the creation of new farm ponds and lakes.

Game Conservancy Limited (Burgate Manor, Fordingbridge, Hampshire, SP6 1EF; Tel 0425 652381; Fax 0425 655848) can give professional and individual advice on the siting, shape, size, depth, location and subsequent management of a farm pond or lake for both conservation and sporting use.

CHAPTER TWO

The Game Conservancy's Wetlands Research at the ARC Wildfowl Centre

The ARC Wildfowl Centre and Reserve

A great deal of the information on wetland habitat creation, improvement and management contained in this publication has arisen from the results of research and management work undertaken by staff of The Game Conservancy's Wetlands Research Unit at the ARC Wildfowl Centre which is at Great Linford, near Milton Keynes in north Buckinghamshire.

This Centre and reserve is owned by ARC Limited – Britain's leading supplier of natural aggregates – who also financed the wetland research which was carried out by The Game Conservancy Trust.

It is an excellent example of industrial and conservation organisations working together to create productive new habitats for wildlife on the new wetlands created by gravel extraction. Research in the 1960s by The Game Conservancy had shown that detailed scientific investigation was necessary to establish the reasons for the unusually low levels of waterfowl production that had been observed on restored gravel pits.

ARC approached The Game Conservancy in 1972 with an offer of practical help by financing a research project. The 300ha Linford gravel pit complex was chosen for this study because it was already used by relatively large numbers of wintering wildfowl, while a 30ha area encompassing one large lake and a number of smaller ones was seen to have the best potential for the creation of a breeding sanctuary and winter refuge.

The project developed steadily, with the establishment of a very rich and attractive wildfowl reserve and the accumulation of much detailed information on gravel pit ecology and waterfowl populations. In 1980 ARC decided to construct a permanent research centre at Great Linford. The ARC Wildfowl Centre was opened in 1982 by The Rt Hon Michael Heseltine MP, the then Secretary of State for the Environment. The Centre has a spacious, well equipped laboratory, a workshop and a fine conference room with a display area, excellent audio visual facilities, seating for 50 people and an observation gallery giving a panoramic view over the reserve. This man-made area now supports a large breeding waterfowl community and attracts significant numbers of wintering ducks, geese and waders.

A total of 189 different bird species (70 of them breeding), 284 species of flowering plants and numerous species of moths, butterflies, dragonflies, other insects, mammals, fish and amphibians have been recorded on site, giving an indication of its great value to wildlife, in addition to the waterfowl. The Game Conservancy's research objectives at Linford were fulfilled by 1992 when the laboratory reverted to ARC management. The final report, 'Wildlife After Gravel', was launched by Lord Crickhowell (Chairman of the National Rivers Authority) on 7 December 1992.

The reserve demonstrates that man-made waters can be made to provide ideal habitats for the conservation of many species of wildlife, even when they are close to a large urban development such as Milton Keynes. The creation and management of this reserve has provided an excellent opportunity to investigate, develop, practise, monitor and demonstrate wetland habitat creation and management techniques appropriate to all man-made and natural freshwaters.

Conservation of habitats and of species is today aided by scientific research; this gives the degree of understanding necessary to formulate conservation strategies for particular habitats. The primary aim of the ARC Wildfowl Centre was therefore to carry out research into the ecology of gravel pits and to collect data on the precise habitat requirements of their waterfowl populations. Through this work, new and more effective techniques are devised for the restoration of gravel pits and other ponds and lakes to create highly productive, attractive habitats for wetland species.

Most of the research effort at the Centre was applied to the study of the factors which control waterfowl breeding success, principally of mallard, tufted duck, Canada and greylag geese. Dietary studies, field observations and the radio-tracking of females and their young have revealed a great deal about their selection of habitats, and the influence of habitat quality on the production of fledged young. It has been shown that the supply of aquatic invertebrates, particularly midges, as food for ducklings is absolutely essential. This was found to be deficient in new man-made waters, and this deficiency was considered to be the cause of the unusually high duckling mortality.

Freshwater fish also rely on the same invertebrate food resource and the research has shown that the diets of perch, bream and tench in particular overlap with that of waterfowl, especially during the spring and summer breeding season. The results suggest that where food supply is limited by environmental factors, the foraging fish can suppress waterfowl production level.

Following the removal of the major part of the fish (mainly bream, roach, tench, perch and pike) from the reserve, the population of larval midges increased fourfold and many new invertebrate species colonised the main lake. This was partly due to the fact that the growth of submerged aquatic plants in the main lake increased enormously in the summer after fish removal, thus providing a greatly improved habitat for invertebrate life. However, amongst these new species were many forms of predatory invertebrate (alder flies, damselflies, dragonflies), previously absent due to fish predation and lack of suitable habitat, and to some extent these reduced the important midge populations in much the same way as the fish did. Of great benefit to tufted ducklings was the population explosion of aquatic snails promoted by the fish removal. It seems likely that the roach were eating virtually all the snails before the fish removal.

Work has also been completed to examine the population dynamics of pike, which although known to be occasional predators of young waterfowl, may regulate other fish populations, thus making more food available for the birds.

The loss of eggs, sitting ducks and ducklings to mammalian and avian predators (foxes, mink and carrion crows for example) is a very frequent occurrence and the effects of this are recorded as part of a long term monitoring programme on the fate of waterfowl nests and broods in the study area.

The educational role of the Wildfowl Centre

The Wildfowl Centre has an important role to play in increasing public awareness of the conservation value of man-made water bodies, including gravel pits, and it is already a well-used resource for environmental education. This aspect of the Wildfowl Centre's work is currently being expanded. Many parties of school children, university students, landowners, farmers, constructionists, wildfowlers, planners and quarry operators, visit the Centre.

Through the publication of scientific papers, articles and books such as this, the ARC Wildfowl Centre has established a national and international reputation as a research unit which is unique in its concentration on the ecology and development of the wildlife potential of gravel pits and man-made wetlands.

In 1986 the Gravel Pit Ecology Research Group was established through the Wildfowl Centre. The aim of this is to develop and encourage contact between universities, colleges, water authorities, voluntary and statutory conservation bodies, County, District and Local Councils and other parties or individuals who have an interest in gravel pits, freshwater ecology and wildfowl. Group members have a wide range of interests and expertise in these fields and the group has a liaison function, increasing the exchange of information on ecological research in gravel pits and encouraging the application of research results to find practical solutions to gravel pit restoration problems, which are also relevant to other wetlands and their management. Thanks to 20 years of Game Conservancy research, the ARC Wildfowl Centre is now able to provide an information bank on environmental science which ARC and other aggregate companies can call upon when needed. This should ensure that more high quality site restoration plans will be made available in future.

CHAPTER THREE

Providing Habitats for Wildfowl

For an area of water to be of maximum benefit to a wide range of wildfowl and other wetland species, it needs to have a number of basic features. This chapter should help the reader to establish what they are, and what is possible on a particular site, to decide where and how to make new ponds and lakes and to ensure that they contain the range of habitats necessary if they are to be useful for wildfowl.

Pond or Lake?

There is often some disagreement as to when a pond becomes a lake. A simple ecological definition which separates ponds from lakes is that a pond is usually shallow enough for submerged rooted aquatic plants to grow over its entire area, ie sunlight can reach the bottom even at the deepest point, while a lake has areas of water too deep for sunlight penetration to the bed and so has a dark (aphotic) zone where there is no plant growth. It is clear, therefore, that the area of the water surface is not the deciding factor; one could have a large area of shallow water as a pond, or a small, very deep area as a lake, but in practice once even shallow water reaches 2–3ha in area it is usually thought of as a lake and similarly, very deep waters which are less than this are generally thought of as a pond! Throughout this book the term "pond" is used in its widest sense, and does not necessarily refer only to the smaller waters. If "lake" is used it usually refers to a very large, deeper water body.

Size of water body for wildfowl

We are frequently asked "How big should the pond be?" – the answer is usually "as big as you can make it"! This is because a larger water is usually more attractive to wintering wildfowl (especially pochard) than a small one. As a general rule, as pond size increases the number of birds using it will increase, but not necessarily in direct proportion. As pond size increases you will have more birds per pond but less birds per acre, thus, a 1ha pond will not hold twice as many birds as 0.5ha pond.

We suggest an absolute minimum size for a farm pond of 0.1–0.2ha (1/4–1/2 acre) and this only if it is fairly close to a larger water body or river that waterfowl use. Waterfowl breeding on ponds of less than one acre in size may suffer disproportionately from the effects of predators attracted from the surrounding land, although the provision of islands as nesting sites helps to reduce this. Small flight ponds of the 0.1 to 0.2ha size do have the advantage of being easier to manage from a shooting point of view.

Water depths required

The next question is usually "How deep?" For dabbling ducks (eg mallard, pintail and teal) we would recommend a range of 15cm to 2.0m with an average depth of 45cm – so most of the pond area would be shallow, with a few deeper holes. On large ponds, where diving ducks (eg tufted duck and pochard) are expected, the depth over most of the pond should be 60cm to 2.5m with an average depth of 1.1m. A large area of water more than 1.7m deep is not good for breeding waterfowl, but is required if fish are to be considered.

If trout are to be stocked, then it is advisable to include places which are at least 2.5–3.0m deep. This is particularly important if the water body is ever to be used as an irrigation supply, when draw down will reduce the level at a time when the shallow water is likely to be warm. In this case a deep channel is needed, to provide at least 2m of water as a fish haven at the fully drawn down level.

Another way to safeguard fish stocks, plant and invertebrate life in waters which suffer from draw down is to construct a bund around a shallow section of the reservoir, this will be submerged at normal water level, but will retain a water filled pool behind it as the level falls.

Shape and shore profiles

The part of the pond where the water is naturally shallow and thus productive is the margin, and for this reason a long, wavy, irregular shoreline, with a very gentle gradient, is much better than a straight shore at a uniformly steep gradient. Similarly, it is a very good idea to leave the graded shores in a rough, lumpy state, not (as is all to often done) have the machine operator comb and smooth down all of the graded surfaces. When flooded the water will soon iron out the minor irregularities and the major ones will add interesting variety to the underwater topography, producing a greater diversity of micro-habitats and thus a greater potential in the pond for species richness to develop.

It may not be a good idea to grade all shores of the pond to a gentle slope. For example, if there is space around the pond it may be possible to build in some vertical earth cliffs, rising straight up from the water and if these are 1.0–2.0m high, they will probably be used by sand martins and kingfishers. For sand martins, unless the cliff face is of a compacted sandy soil, it will be necessary to lay in sections of plastic drainpipe packed with sand which is held in place by a small crescent shaped fillet of cement at the mouth of the pipe. The pipes should be laid level and should be perforated at intervals along the base to allow for drainage.

Underwater substrates

The soil or substrate of the bed of the pond or lake has enormous influence on its biological productivity and conservation value. In this context, the underwater substrates have more far-reaching effects on the value of the water body to wildfowl than the soils of the banks.

As a general principle, the texture and nature of the substrate of the pond should be made as varied as possible. This is because different plants and animals have preferences for different types of soil. Some prefer sand, silt, clay or loamy soils while others like it to be rocky, stony or gravelly. Thus, the wider the variety of substrate, the greater the diversity of plants and animals the area will support, thereby creating a richer, more interesting and more stable ecosystem.

This variety in underwater habitats should be made during the construction work by covering some parts of the pond bed with a 15–20cm layer of clean gravel and/or sand, with silt or mud in the hollows; large limestone boulders can be used to create reefs in a variety of water depths. Such reefs are extremely valuable for fish and, if they break the surface, will be used by roosting wildfowl.

A problem with newly excavated waters is that they are ecologically immature. The substrate usually lacks the organic matter essential as food for the many organisms which form the base of the food chain for fish and wildfowl. Over a long period the water will accumulate an organic sediment derived from the remains of aquatic plant and animal life, and the number of different organisms and their total productivity will increase. This, however, can take a great many years and various techniques may be used to overcome this time lag.

Whenever possible the lake or pond bed should be treated before the water is allowed in. The topsoil should be stripped and stored separately (in low heaps, less than 1m deep, as this reduces soil deterioration) so that it may eventually be spread on the dry lake bed in a 15–20cm layer. This provides a good plant rooting medium with a high level of plant nutrients, and also provides a better habitat for the important aquatic animals such as midge larvae, which like to burrow in lake sediments. Being organically enriched with humus, topsoil also contains much more food for such animals than the hard-panned bed of most new excavations and so this layer of topsoil gives the whole cycle of productivity an enormous boost right at the start. Where the water supply for a new pond or lake is nutrient-rich (containing nitrates, phosphates) then, in order to avoid over-enrichment, it is better to use subsoil, rather than topsoil.

What do wildfowl need?

Once the basin of a new water body has been constructed to include the features described above, it will need several modifications if it is to be fully utilised by wildfowl. This next section details the range of habitat types and features that are needed within a wetland to maximise its value for conservation. It examines the seasonal requirements of wildfowl and describes ways in which those needs can be catered for, looking at the need for seclusion, good conditions for nesting, brood rearing and feeding and for safe loafing and moulting sites. The details apply equally to the improvement of existing wetlands.

Ideally the site should not only attract wildfowl in the winter, when all they are looking for is a safe, quiet roosting and/or feeding site, and when you can shoot it occasionally as a flight pond, but it should also provide for the needs of some breeding birds, so that you maintain a local waterfowl population, thereby "putting something back". It can be enormously satisfying to follow the progress of "your" ducklings on your own pond, and naturally produced birds like this are likely to be far more valuable to the population as a whole than hand reared ones.

Taking each of the waterfowl requirements in turn we will look first at the need for undisturbed habitats.

Seclusion and Shelter

One of the primary requirements of a good wildfowl area is freedom from disturbance, particularly in the breeding season between February and July. Human disturbance is a major factor influencing the use of any habitat by wild waterfowl and it must be kept to a minimum. No matter how good the habitat may be, it will not be fully used if it is regularly disturbed by random human intrusion. To a degree, wild birds will learn to tolerate regular visits, especially of vehicles – provided their occupants remain inside – but even this should be kept to a low level. Any recreational use will need to be confined to specific zones, away from the best habitats.

The siting of ponds is therefore important; it should be well away from houses, roads, farm buildings, footpaths etc. and of course not directly under overhead power lines. A stout perimeter fence and a wide, preferably thorny, hedge is almost essential around the water. These will keep out people and livestock.

A very effective barrier which we developed at the ARC gravel pit site at Great Linford is the security canal. This is a 3–4m wide moat dug to surround and isolate the breeding sanctuary and the north western and western shores of the main lake from the mainland. This canal has a deep outer section, with a shallow wet shelf to support the growth of reeds or rushes on the inner side (Figure 1).

This canal therefore forms additional habitat and grows a screen, as well as fulfilling its security function. If this technique is used, the spoil from the moat should be used to create a bank on the inner side. The canal prevents people climbing the bank and the reeds hide it from the outer side. The screening and shelter provided by such a system is extremely good and can be further enhanced by planting the bank with a suitable evergreen and thorny shrub such as gorse.

Tree and shrub planting can be used to increase the seclusion of a wildfowl breeding area, providing a visual barrier, screening paths and tracks, giving shelter from the wind and considerably increasing the value of the site to wildlife. The presence of a range of native

Figure 1. A canal and bank around a pond make it very secluded.

15

trees and shrubs adds considerably to the variety of habitats and thus increases the number of bird and insect species present. Trees around ponds are, however, often a source of problems. The shade cast by trees overhanging the waterside reduces the growth of the water plants, so they can be used to retain some open water areas alongside the shore if planted on the south side. But this must not be overdone as too much shade will reduce the productivity of the water body and the autumn leaf fall will add large amounts of leaf litter to the water, resulting in possible over enrichment and stagnation.

As a general rule, tree planting should be at least 30m (or 1.5m × tree height) away from the waterside to reduce leaf fall into the water and to allow a better flight lines in and out for the ducks. The more open skyline close to the water also makes flight shooting much easier. It is a good plan to plant a tree shelter belt around a pond in four zones, using taller tree species just inside the outer perimeter fence and hedge, with moderate height trees inside these, grading into a belt of lower growing trees and then shrubs towards

Zones: A   B   C   D

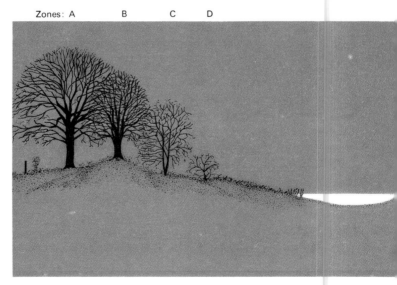

Figure 2. Tree and shrub shelter belts round a pond need to be carefully planne

the waterside (see Figure 2). A similar gradation of edges outwards would also help to enhance the value of the belt for other game and wildlife. If the belt of land available for planting is too narrow to allow this, it is usually best to leave out Zone A and have a lower first height.

Outer Zone – A (tall species)	Middle Zone – B (medium height)	Inner Zone – C (small trees)	Shrub Zone – D (low shrubs)
Scots pine	Common oak	Spindle tree	Wayfaring tree
Beech	Sessile oak	Rowan	Barberry
Black poplar	Hornbeam	Hazel	Box
Grey poplar	Alder	Aspen	Blackthorn
White willow	Silver birch	Hawthorn	Broom
Common lime	Downy birch	Alder buckthorn	Gorse
Small leaved lime	Crack willow	Purging buckthorn	Wild privet
Ash	Whitebeam	Holly	Dog rose
	Wych elm	Goat willow	Bramble
	Wild cherry	Osier willow	Dogwood
	Bird cherry	Elder	Guelder rose
		Field maple	
		Crab apple	

These features are also shown on Figure 3, the illustration of the "ideal" pond.

We recommend the use of native species of tree and shrub for all sites where wildlife conservation is the primary objective and the lists above give a selection of native species of tree and shrub suitable for each zone. The Arboricultural Association publishes a list of trees suitable for a wide range of soil types and locations, and Game Conservancy Advisors can also help to select suitable species following a site visit.

The correct preparation of the site before tree planting is vital if they are to grow successfully. Good drainage is essential and therefore any soil compaction resulting from the use of heavy plant in the construction of the water body must be corrected. Deep cultivation with a winged-tine subsoiler is best if there is any form of soil pan. Details of tree planting plans and specifications will vary with each site and The Game Conservancy's Advisors are able to help with such plans. If your pond is constructed by building an earth dam, do not plant trees on this as they are liable to undermine it as they grow.

Habitat for breeding wildfowl

Several studies have shown that the availability of nest sites is one factor which can limit the size of the breeding population of wildfowl, and fortunately it is relatively simple to meet the requirements for good nesting conditions.

Given an adequate degree of security, breeding ducks' main need is for good nest cover and access to insect-rich brood rearing areas. The cover is essential to provide concealment for the nests and therefore to reduce losses to predators. As far as possible, the invertebrate-rich shallow waters essential for brood rearing should be close to the nest sites. Our research has shown that the further a mallard brood has to travel from nest to brood rearing site, the greater is the mortality within that brood.

Wildfowl will be more inclined to use the pond for breeding if it also provides escape cover and open loafing spots for use during their annual moult. A long, convoluted shoreline provides a greater "edge" and more possible choices of nest site, particularly for species like tufted duck which nest close to the water.

Predators and nesting wildfowl

Unless their activities are limited, some birds and mammals will much reduce the number of successful nests of ground-nesting species of waterfowl. Carrion crows, magpies, jackdaws (and, on occasions, rooks, moorhens and coot), foxes, mink, rats and occasionally stoats and squirrels will all take the eggs of ducks, while foxes and crows can also eat goose eggs. These predators will also, of course, reduce the nesting success of many other songbird and game species.

If the eggs of a nesting bird are eaten they will obviously never hatch and the potential production of that female in that year may be totally lost. If it was an early nest there is a good chance that the bird may re-nest, producing a second clutch of eggs, but this is dependent upon a very good supply of protein-rich invertebrate food for her, and even then second clutches tend to be smaller, with poorer quality eggs. If the nest was taken later in the season the female is very likely to go straight into eclipse (the annual feather moult) and thus fail to breed at all that year.

The majority of egg predators are also quite capable of taking the young birds when they have hatched, and so again the year's production will suffer. In many cases the adult bird will be killed, particularly if found by a fox or mink when she is close to hatching the eggs and is thus reluctant to abandon them and waste all of the materials, energy and time that she has invested in the nest. When this happens, that bird's potential for production of young is gone for ever!

It is clear, then, that uncontrolled losses of nesting females, eggs and young birds to predators can have a really significant effect in reducing the number of waterfowl and other bird species using your

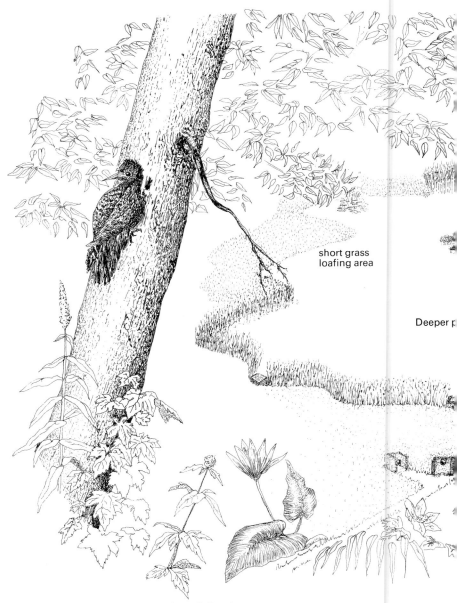

short grass
loafing area

Deeper p

Figure 3. The "idealised" pond for wildfowl.

20

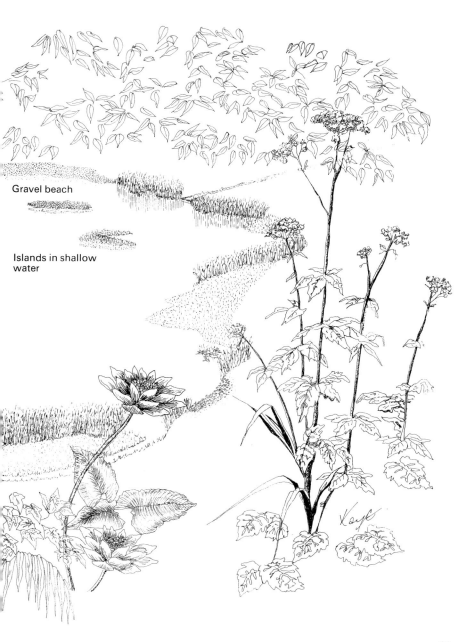

Gravel beach

Islands in shallow
water

21

pond or lake for breeding. These losses can be severe enough to limit the size of the local population, as well as reducing any surplus production that you may wish to harvest during the shooting season, so it is definitely worthwhile attempting to mitigate the effects of predators.

If you are expending time and resources on the creation and management of a pond or lake in order to increase the number of wildfowl, it is frustrating to see your efforts going to feed the local predators. It is essential to consider the local population of nest predators (ie only those which are legally considered to be pest species) as a factor in the habitat which is as open to management as any other, and steps can be taken to limit their impact on nesting waterfowl.

The impact of predators can be mitigated in two ways:

1. The most obvious and very effective way is to make a concerted effort to kill predators over a fairly wide area around the water body by all of the legal means for a short period starting in February, just before the nesting season, and ending after the ducklings are fledged in July. This causes a local reduction in predator density, thus reducing their food requirements and relieving pressure on the nests and young of the waterfowl.

Some of the predators removed will be replaced by immigrants moving in from outside the controlled area, so the effort needs to be continuous, with daily checking of all traps and snares. The new-comers need to be removed soon after they arrive, but even if this takes some days they will be to some extent naïve, not knowing the area as well as the previous residents, and so they are likely to be much less efficient at hunting it.

In any programme of predator reduction it is essential to consider the total local predator population as almost a single entity, and to attempt to effect a reduction of all of them as far as the law allows. It is widely known among gamekeepers, and more recently from scientific studies by The Game Conservancy Trust, that if only one component of the full spectrum of predators is removed (foxes for example), then the proportion of nests taken by one of the other predators whose numbers are not controlled will be greater, because predators are efficient and opportunistic and more nests remain to be found.

Those readers who require more information on techniques and the law relating to predator control are referred to The Game Conservancy's Guide No 7, Predator and Squirrel Control.

2. The second way of limiting the impact of nest predators is the provision of first class nesting and brood rearing habitats in and around the pond. In order to maximise the effect this should be coupled with a local reduction of predator density in spring and early summer as described above. However, for those who find it unacceptable, or have no desire, to control the predator numbers, the provision of first class habitat is essential to achieve any degree of nesting success for the local waterfowl. As an additional measure in the case of the smaller farm pond or lake, it could be feasible to protect the nesting birds from foxes by surrounding the entire area with electrified sheep netting during the breeding season, but the foxes have been known to jump over it!

The importance of good nest cover

The following section describes the features essential for the development of a successful population of nesting waterfowl.

Nesting, ducks prefer tall, tussocky herbaceous plants eg tussock grasses, sedges, rushes, nettles, willowherb, cow parsley etc., and also shrubby cover such as provided by brambles, dogwoods, gorse, and coppice willow, in a situation where they are safe from predators. Mallard in particular nest early in the season, often before new growth begins, so the dead stems of plants like nettles and willow herb from the previous season are invaluable in providing some cover for these early nests.

Figure 4 shows the relationship between nest cover height and nest predation in mallard.

This type of cover can best be provided by allowing the natural flora to develop from the seed bank in the soil of the land around the water body and on the islands. Where the natural herbaceous

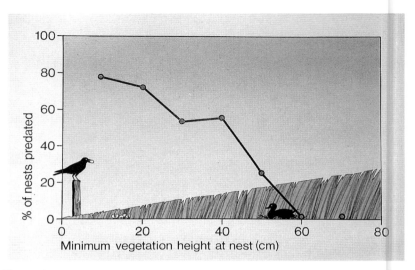

Figure 4. Nest losses to predators are reduced by the provision of tall, dense ground cover for nest concealment.

flora is allowed to develop in this way as nesting habitat, it should be cut, grazed hard, or burned off every three to five years. Left longer than this, the quality of the nest cover deteriorates as trees invade and scrub begins to develop. This should be prevented, as ducks generally prefer not to nest under dense tree shade. For the same reasons, one should also avoid planting too many trees on nesting islands and in the areas of mainland cover intended for duck nesting. Remember that trees are best kept more than 30 metres from the pond, planted as a sheltering screen. Failing this they should be kept bushy by regular coppicing.

Use of wildflower mixtures

The underlying theme of this book is the creation of habitats important to wildfowl conservation, and as such it is specifically about watery sites. However, it is not only wetlands that we have lost in

24

Britain. Since 1945, the tremendous scale of wetland loss has been matched by that of old herb-rich grasslands. The development of such herb-rich swards around a farm pond or lake therefore has much to commend it, and such habitats can be very attractive visually, whilst at the same time acting as valuable nest cover. Selected blocks of land should be seeded with a suitable wildflower meadow mixture as soon as landscaping is completed. In this case it is important not to spread topsoil on these areas, as plant diversity and establishment will be best on nutrient-poor soils.

Mixtures of seed from native species should be used and many of these are now available commercially. Detailed advice on the composition of grass-herb mixtures for different soils and purposes can be found in a Nature Conservancy Council (NCC) publication, "Creating attractive grasslands using native plant species".

Sowing of such mixtures must be in fairly fine, firm seed beds made by harrowing and rolling the rotavated area under dry conditions, ideally in September. The bed should be weed-free; if it is already vegetated this should be sprayed off with glyphosate, checking first that there are no rare species present. A light raking or harrowing should follow seed sowing, then the area should be lightly rolled.

To establish rapid vegetation cover and prevent soil erosion on low fertility soils it is advisable to sow a nurse crop with the grass-herb mixture. Westerwolds rye grass is recommended as it germinates quickly and eventually dies out, allowing the slower growing, more permanent species to replace it. On fertile soils, the wildflower/grass mix should be sown alone, as a nurse crop would soon swamp it.

Competition from docks and thistles can be a problem on recently disturbed soils, and management after germination of the seed mixture is important. There should be a first light cut at 10cm, about 6–8 weeks after sowing, and the cut material must be removed. This allows the herbs in the lower layers to develop with the grasses, but reduces the competition from taller weeds and/or the nurse crop. Cutting every two months throughout the first season will help the cover establish, with a final cut in late October. Once established, the meadows can be mown annually after the nesting season ends, always removing the cut material.

Although desirable, it is not absolutely necessary to ensure good nest cover right next to the pond, provided it exists reasonably close by. In many cases if the pond is good for feeding and brood rearing, but does not have good nesting conditions around it, mallard will nest some distance away – perhaps at the base of a hedge or ditch bank, or in the edge of a copse up to a kilometre away – and will bring their broods to the pond to rear them. This is particularly so if there is a stream or ditch joining the next cover to the pond, hence the importance of siting the pond so that it is linked to other habitats.

Predators can find nests more easily in thin strips of cover, so the nesting areas should be made in large blocks or patches, not just as an encircling strip round the water's edge. Additional nest sites can be provided in the form of floating rafts, nest baskets or boxes.

The value of islands for nesting

Islands are very definitely preferred by wildfowl as nest sites. They suffer less from disturbance than mainland sites, they are surrounded by water, therefore offering easy escape and chances of good feeding, and they are not normally accessible to grazing livestock, so have better nest cover. Nest losses to predators are usually less on islands.

The shape, size and position of the islands will influence the extent to which waterfowl use them.

The shallow littoral (shore) is the most productive part of the wetland ecosystem, and so it is important to try to make islands with as long a shoreline as possible. A basic rectangular shaped island of a certain area has a longer perimeter than a square one of the same area, which in turn is longer around than a circular one. So, it is best to make the islands in some form of irregular elongated shape to maximise the productive waterline habitat.

26

If islands are made in the shape of a horseshoe, with the mouth almost closed, they can enclose a shallow lagoon, giving extra shelter and security (Figure 5).

Alternatively, if made in the shape of a Maltese cross, a shallow bay can be made in each of the four angles giving some sheltered water whichever way the wind is blowing (Figure 6.)

Evidence from several studies shows that there is a positive correlation between both wildfowl nest density and nest hatching success on an island and its distance offshore. In practice the ideal minimum distance was found to be 170m, but it is accepted that (with the exception of gravel pits) this will not generally be possible in the sort of ponds and lakes that we are discussing in this book. It is a good general principle, however, that islands are best if sited well away from the shore (at least 10 metres).

This requirement to make the islands as far offshore as possible should not be used as the reason to crowd them all together in the

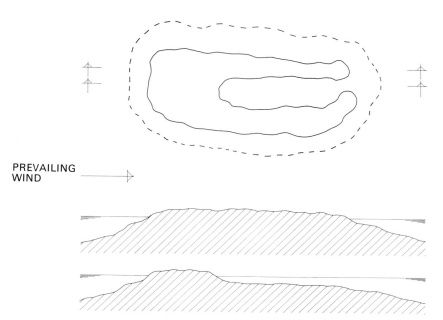

PREVAILING WIND

Figure 5. A "horseshoe" island can enclose a shallow, sheltered lagoon.

27

centre of the pool. Ideally, they will be more or less evenly scattered. This is because nest losses to predators which can reach the island (crows, mink and sometimes foxes) have been shown to be greater where islands are aggregated. The 'clumps' of islands provide a locally increased density of nests, making it easier for the searching predators to find a greater proportion of them.

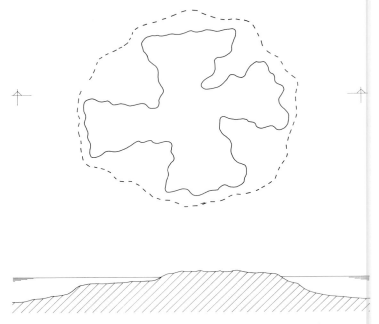

Figure 6. A "Maltese Cross" island will provide good sheltered water areas in any wind direction.

It has also been shown that nest density is inversely correlated with island size, and so provided they are of a certain minimum size, a number of smaller islands will hold more nests per acre than one large one which covers the same total area. The islands should be at least 5m wide, preferably 10m, and the ideal minimum area is 0.1ha, say 20m wide by 50m long, but again it is recognised that this is only possible in larger waters.

28

Construction of islands

If you are fortunate enough to be making a new pond by one of the methods described in Chapter 6, you can build in the islands as part of the construction process. Provided the work has been planned correctly, the final water level will be known and spoil heaps can be raised in the appropriate spots, with their tops profiled to be flat or with very gentle gradients only (ducks and geese will not nest on slopes steeper than about 1 in 4; even the cliff-nesting species like barnacle geese must find a level platform on which to build). Unless they are to be planted with a wildflower mixture, islands should be surfaced with topsoil not planted with trees, and should not be seeded with grass. The germination from the seed bank will quickly provide good nest cover.

If the pond or lake is already water filled, and it is either not possible or not desirable to drain it, islands can still be made, provided it is possible to bring suitable inert infill material to the site. This should be subsoil, builders' rubble etc, and in many areas there is a demand for sites in which to dispose of such material. The infill must not, of course, contain any hazardous or potentially polluting material. Also if the site is operated as a temporary local tip to obtain the infill (and this can be very profitable), it will be essential to obtain planning permission if the material is imported from outside the holding.

The material is dumped on the water's edge near the point where the island is to be made. It is then pushed out, using a mechanical digger, into the water to form a promontory or peninsula, which the machine consolidates as it progresses out into the water. The shoreward end of the peninsula should be kept as narrow as possible because this is eventually to be cut through, making a channel to isolate the rest of the infill as a new island. If the peninsula is made long and irregular in shape and direction, it can be "chopped" into a number of islands, like a string of beads (Figure 7).

The soil dug out of the channels between the new islands is placed in the water on the island shores to make extra shallow, productive feeding habitat.

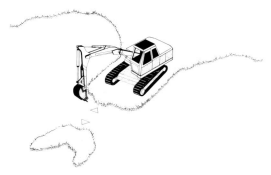

Figure 7. Islands can be made without de-watering a lake by using suitable infill material.

Should you have a water with a number of existing peninsulas along the shoreline, it is a good idea to cut these off by a water channel, to make them better as nest sites.

If they are in exposed situations, the island shores will need to be protected by the establishment of a fringe of emergent aquatic plants, using the techniques described in Chapter 4, or by means of floating pole wave baffles, rip-rap or some other form of stone cladding on the waterline.

If the water is less than 1m deep it is possible to make islands by placing concrete pipe rings vertically in the water and filling the core with packed straw, rubble, earth etc, but these do not look in any way natural. Similar but better looking islands can be made in shallow water by driving in willow stakes to make the island outline. These then have willow rods woven between them and the inside is filled in with rubble, earth or packed straw. If the stakes are used when fresh cut in the dormant season they will grow, fringing the island with willows which, although they look attractive, need to be cut back each autumn. It is usually found that willows planted into standing water die out after a few years, but by then the consolidated islands should remain.

Straw bale stacks fixed with stakes can also be used to build semi-permanent islands in shallow sheltered locations, but the bales need to be thoroughly waterlogged before being placed together. Big round or square bales can be used singly to make small islands in water of suitable depth. If placed so that the surface of the bales is only just above the water level and the spot is sheltered by over-hanging trees, such bale islands are very attractive to nesting grebes, moorhens and coots.

Artificial islands on rafts

If it is not possible to create real islands, additional safe nest sites can be provided by mooring large, stable rafts on the pond. These should have a layer of turf laid on them so that natural plant cover will grow up, they can be shingle covered for nesting terns and plovers, or they may be provided with nest boxes or baskets. Unlike fixed nest boxes, those on rafts have the advantage that they can rise and fall with changing water levels. Raft islands are also valu-able as open water roosting or loafing sites outside the breeding season, and they can be positioned to bring wild birds closer to observation hides for birdwatchers.

Raft islands need to be fairly substantial to withstand the effects of constant motion on the water and also the larger the raft the more stable it will be. They must also have a dry upper surface because, surprising as it may seem, most waterfowl prefer a dry base to their nests. This means that the raft should include the provision of some form of gently sloping "boarding ramp" leading down into the water to give easier access.

For small sheltered ponds the raft can be relatively small, pro-vided it is at least 1.3m square. A simple design for a very effective small raft is shown in Figure 8.

The raft is basically a box-like framework of 150×25mm boards, open at the top and bottom, surrounding a smaller, inner box of the same material, and this inner one has a boarded-over top to form the surface of the raft. The inner box has two of its sides formed by cross-members running between two sides of the outer box and the outer box is linked to the inner one with short lengths of 125×15mm wood, making a series of compartments around the

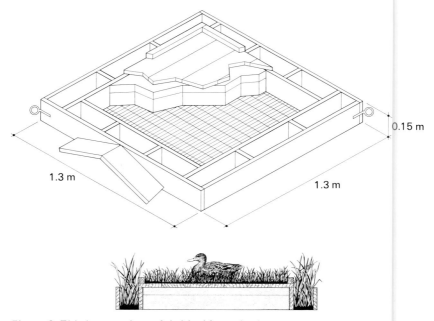

0.15 m

1.3 m

1.3 m

Figure 8. This box section raft is ideal for a single nest.

centre of the raft. This centre portion contains expanded polystyrene
sheets (building insulation material) which are held in place by a
sheet of galvanised or plastic netting stapled to the underside of
the raft. This netting also serves as an open floor to the compartments around the raft and these are planted with clumps of rushes
(*Juncus spp.*) which are cut to fit.

For open waters the same design can be used, but made much
larger. A very substantial raft can easily be made using old telegraph
or electricity poles; these are heavy, strong and very durable, and
usually available quite cheaply from British Telecom or the local
electricity company's engineering department.

The method we have devised and tested is very simple; it is shown
in Figure 9.

Cut two poles to the chosen length and lay them parallel on level
ground close to the water. Join the poles together with stout angle

32

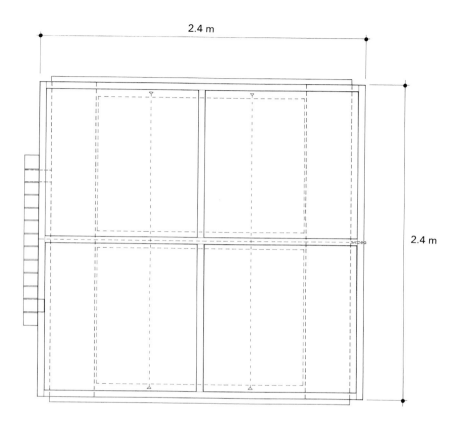

2.4 m

2.4 m

Figure 9. For larger waters, and for more nests, this more substantial telegraph pole raft is better.

iron or strong planking, fastened to the cut end of each pole using two 150 × 13mm coach screws at each end.

Then fix a sheet of 100mm thick expanded polystyrene building insulation to a sheet or sheets, depending on the raft size, of marine or exterior grade 13mm plywood, lacing it into position with plastic covered wire and staples. This is necessary to provide the buoyancy as the poles themselves will not be sufficient, and they will eventually absorb enough water to make them unable to support the raft.

The plywood sheet(s) are then laid (polystyrene side down) on top of the poles to form the raft surface, being fastened into position with galvanised or copper nails, or better still a number of coach screws.

The perimeter of the raft surface is formed and reinforced by nailing a 50 × 25mm strip of wood around the edge, on top of the plywood. This is necessary to retain the thin layer of soil and turf which is later placed on the raft *after* it has been launched – it will be too heavy to move if it is added while still on the shore. The surface of the plywood can be covered with a layer of 13mm mesh wire netting to give the turf something to bind to, and the turf layer can similarly be held in place by another layer of wire mesh. As an alternative, a thick layer of wet straw can be fixed to the raft surface with wire mesh, and this will eventually be colonised by plant cover.

The raft should be equipped with wooden ramps sloping down into the water to allow easy access by ducklings. If the aim is to cater for breeding terns, ringed and little ringed plover, the plywood surface of the raft should be divided into a number of small, shallow compartments or cells, by nailing stripwood across it in both directions, so that a layer of gravelly soil can be placed on the raft surface and the stripwood grid will help to hold it in place during windy weather. Without them the gravel slides to one end, the raft tips, and the gravel ends up on the bottom of the pond! Rafts for terns should be allowed to grow a thin scattering of vegetation to give cover for the chicks, otherwise they abandon ship at the first sign of danger, and tern rafts also need boarding ramps.

The raft will need to have two mooring points. These should be holes made in a very stout piece of steel fastened securely to each

34

end of the raft, ideally to both of the poles. The mooring lines must be really strong; we use multi-stranded flexible wire rope, with a circumference of 19mm and a breaking strain of 4050kg. This is fastened at each end using Bulldog Clips to a short length of 25mm chain. The end of one of these pieces of chain is shackled firmly to the mooring eye on the raft and the end of the other is attached to the anchor. The anchor can be any object with sufficient weight and small bulk, but it is probably best to make them from concrete. The simplest way to do this is to lay the end of the mooring chain into a large plastic tub, such as a cut down 25 litre drum, which is then filled with concrete (Figure 10).

If an additional smaller weight is slid down to a stop about half way down the mooring wire, its weight will put a greater curve into the mooring line. This device is known to mariners as an "angel", and it increases the efficiency of the anchor by lowering the angle of pull on the anchor and by acting as a "spring" to reduce chafe and snatching on the chain and line in rough weather (Figure 11).

The anchors can be placed on the raft, attached with a suitable length of mooring line and the raft is floated into position. Once in the appropriate place, they are simply pushed overboard. In exposed waters it is essential to have plenty of scope on the mooring lines, they should be a minimum of 4 × water depth, 6 × depth if the raft is very large.

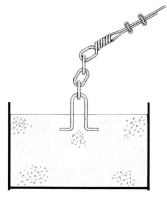

Figure 10. Concrete filled oil-drum bases make good raft anchors.

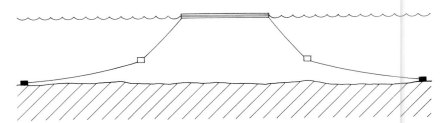

Figure 11. Extra weights ("angels") part way down the mooring lines, will considerably increase raft stability.

Artificial nests

Raft islands are a good place to fix artificial nest structures such as boxes and baskets, and these have some potential for increasing the production of wildfowl. However, their use is really justified only in those sites where there is insufficient natural nest cover, or where success in those sites is very poor as a result of the activities of predators or spring flooding. Artificial nests can have an adverse effect if they attract birds to nest in sites which are incapable of supporting the number of young that will be produced, or where the nesting birds are insufficiently secure from predators. Our observations have shown that hand-reared mallard take to using artificial nests more readily than true wild ones, and there is some evidence that ducklings which hatch within a box or basket are more likely to nest in one later in life.

Nest boxes for dabbling and diving ducks can be made quite cheaply from slabwood and offcuts of timber (Figure 12).

They are simply an open bottomed box whose inside dimensions are 30cm square, 23cm high, with a 15cm square entrance. The roof can be removable to allow easy checking of the nests. A 23–30cm long, 15cm square tunnel should be added to the entrance to prevent access by corvids. They are more likely to be used if the interior is painted black.

Their positioning is very important. They should be placed on a dry level spot, 1m or less from the shoreline, with the funnel facing the water. There should be easy access for the bird from the water

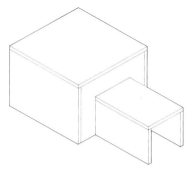

Figure 12. A simple next box for ducks.

at a point opposite the box entrance, and the earth under the box should be scraped away to make a shallow depression which is then lined with a handful of hay. It is also a good idea to sprinkle a simazine-based, or similar persistent herbicide, inside the nest box, otherwise it can rapidly fill with plant growth. Tufted ducks use them only if they are on rafts, or placed on the ground very close to the water's edge, especially on islands.

The Dutch type nesting baskets, introduced by The Game Conservancy Trust, are a little more expensive, but do provide ideal nest sites. Being open weave, the sitting duck can see out, they give good protection from crows and, if they are fixed onto a pole tripod over the water, from foxes and other ground predators. If they are sited on poles over water, the base should be 20–25cm above the water (higher if it is likely to rise) and the funnel entrance should be sloped upwards slightly to allow the duck easier entrance.

If placed in a bed of vegetation the area under the basket should be cleared so that it is over open water, not plants. If they are used on rafts, where we have found them to be more acceptable to wild mallard, they should be at least 1.3m apart and face in opposite directions. If they are closer than this, there is a risk that the nesting female in one basket will desert her eggs and follow the brood from a neighbouring basket if they hatch first. As with boxes, the baskets need a lining of soft dry grass to encourage ducks to use them.

Baskets are best placed in position in January and removed at the end of the season in late August, when they should be emptied, cleaned, treated with a water-based wood preservative and stored under dry conditions. This way they will last almost indefinitely.

It is possible to make artificial nest sites from 25 litre plastic or metal drums, laid on their sides, with entrance holes cut in the end. These are not very attractive however, and should be covered with a thatch of straw or reeds. Metal drums should also be situated in shady spots; in full sun the temperature inside can soon become far too high for both duck and eggs.

Hole nesting species such as shelduck and goldeneye respond well to the provision of artificial nests. Shelduck need a trench about 15cm wide and 30cm deep, dug into a bank for about 40cm, ending in a nest chamber 35cm in diameter. The trench and chamber should be roofed over with boards or inverted turves. Alternatively, a nest chamber can be made by burying a 25 litre drum in an earth bank, sloping it slightly down at the back, with drainage holes made in the base, and a short, level 15–20cm pipe laid and buried to make a tunnel entrance (Figure 13).

Goldeneye are tree nesters and take readily to using nest boxes of a suitable size. Figure 14 shows a simple plywood nest box as developed by the RSPB for this species. However, unless you have hand-reared goldeneye, they are unlikely to remain and nest in southern Britain as they have only started to nest in central Scotland in the last 20 years.

The range of artificial nest structures possible for a variety of

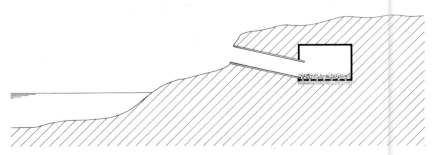

Figure 13. A shelduck nest burrow.

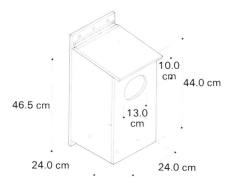

Figure 14. This design of nest box has proved successful for goldeneye.

species is quite considerable and readers who require more detailed information are referred to "Artificial nesting structures for water-birds" by H G Lumsden, Chapter 20, pages 179–199, in "Managing Wetlands and their Birds", published by the International Water-fowl Research Bureau, Slimbridge, Glos. (Ed. D A Scott).

Roosting and loafing sites

Wildfowl spend a relatively high proportion of their time at resting or roosting sites, where they sleep, preen, digest their food and await the time for the next feeding flight. For wintering ducks, this is a daytime habit, as most of them feed at night in the surrounding farmland and in streams, ditches, flashes, small farm ponds and flight ponds etc, which are often disturbed by day. Geese, on the other hand, usually feed during the daylight hours, roosting at night, except during full moons, when the pattern can be reversed, or when they feed by day and by night.

So if wildfowl are to use the new pond or lake to the full, there is a definite need to provide for the needs of resting birds. It is not only necessary that wintering birds have a safe day roost, but the right conditions are particularly important during the mid-summer moult period, when the birds are flightless. Ducklings, too, have a need for dry, bare areas for drying off, preening, being brooded and sleeping, so some suitable places should be made and managed within the breeding area of the pool.

A large, open water body, typical of those produced by gravel pits, forms a suitable roost for much of the time. The essential feature is an extensive area of sheltered water, without any dense beds of emergent aquatic plants, where the birds can remain far from shore in calm conditions.

In a large lake, these conditions are best provided by forming long islands or peninsulas in the lake, with their long axis at 90° to the prevailing wind direction. If possible, these islands should be made so that they have quite a marked upward slope, with the upwind shore at a gradient of about 1 in 4 to 1 in 6, and the downwind side at 1 in 2 to give a high bank with good shelter in its lee. The higher side of the "wind shelter island" can be planted with trees, and thus the island profile deflects the wind upwards to be filtered and slowed by the trees, and gives a larger area of sheltered water downwind (Figure 15).

Ideally, the islands should have a rocky or gravelly shore on the downwind side where the roosting birds can sit in safety. For teal to use it as a roost, the sheltered water area should be only around 3–4cm deep. This little duck loves to roost where it can stand in shallow water, and these conditions will also suit many other species.

If the lake is large enough, the islands can be arranged so that the shelter produced by one overlaps the next island downwind. It is also a good idea to use the wind shelter style of island to protect some of the very shallow, weedy, invertebrate-rich areas that are needed by feeding ducklings; similarly, duck nesting and loafing rafts can be moored in the lee of such islands.

As well as open water day roosts, there is an additional need for shore based resting places, usually referred to as loafing spots. These are particularly valuable in rough weather, when an exposed open water roost loses its appeal, and they are especially valuable during the mid-summer moult period.

Loafing wildfowl (and waders and gulls) show a marked prefer-

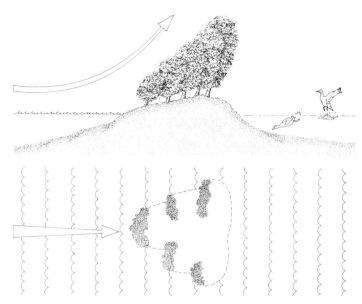

Figure 15. Islands aligned at right angles to the prevailing wind direction pro-vide areas of sheltered water in their lee. Trees help to deflect and slow the wind.

ence for banks with a very short grass sward, or areas of gravel beach with just a sprinkling of vegetation, right next to the extra security of open water. Such loafing spots should be made on shores with a very open aspect, preferably facing south, and a number of the islands should be managed as loafing spots.

What is important is that the loafing birds should feel secure. There must be no tall cover to conceal the approach of predators, no dense reed bed barrier between the bird and the extra security of open water, and they must be in a fairly elevated position to give them a good all-round view of their surroundings.

Suitable sites can be provided most simply by allowing cattle, or preferably sheep, to graze an elevated section of the shore to keep the vegetation short and to remove or reduce any fringe of marginal aquatic plants. The most popular loafing spots are usually narrow peninsulas or islands, where open water is never far away. If possible the loafing spots should be sheltered from the wind and should face towards the south.

If you are building a new pond or lake it is possible to make ideal loafing spots by covering a suitably graded south facing bank with a 500g black polythene sheet, which is then covered over with 20–30cm of 6–18mm gravel. The shore gradient needs to be very gentle or the gravel may slide off the sheet. If the waterline suffers from much wave action, or if the slope is at all steep, it might be necessary to lay a small wall of rough concrete, exposed aggregate paving slabs or suchlike along the waterline to retain the gravel (Figure 16).

The polythene sheet and depth of gravel combine to suppress the growth of any plants, resulting in an almost bare loafing beach. In time this will be colonised by plants, and while a thin scattered covering of vegetation increases the attractiveness of the site to loafing wildfowl (and incidentally to nesting little ringed and ringed plover), it will need to be kept under control by occasional use of a rake or a herbicide such as glyphosate.

During the mid-summer moult period many ducks prefer to hide away in dense beds of vegetation rather than sit out on loafing spots and it is essential to provide some areas around the pond where the water is shallow enough to allow the growth of large beds of plants such as bur-reed.

Ducks also love to climb out of the water and sit on floating poles, logs or old tree trunks and branches laid in the water, and any additional features such as these will help to increase waterfowl use of the pond.

Wildfowl feeding habitat

If the pond or lake is to attract large numbers of water birds of a variety of species during the winter, and if it is to support high densities of breeding birds, it must provide in some measure for their food requirements. This is particularly true if the area is to produce a worthwhile number of fledged young.

Waterfowl can be classified on the basis of their feeding behaviour

Figure 16. A layer of gravel over black polythene sheet makes an ideal wildfowl loafing beach, preferably on an island or peninsula.

as "dabblers" – shallow water surface feeders such as mallard, teal, pintail, gadwall, shoveler; "divers" – underwater feeders such as tufted duck, pochard, goldeneye, smew, goosander, merganser, grebes and true divers (eg great northern); "grazers" – such as the geese, swans, wigeon and coot; "probers" – principally the waders; and "pickers", like moorhen and water rail. Although this gives a broad indication of the different feeding habits that need to be catered for, it is a very simplistic division and there is considerable overlap between the groups; for example, coot will dive to feed and tufted ducks will dabble.

Of the dabbling ducks, gadwall and shoveler are primarily aquatic feeders all year round; pintail and shelduck are largely estuarine feeders and, while teal will feed on land, they do prefer watery sites. Mallard, however, do much of their autumn and winter feeding on farmland. Waste field crops such as wheat, barley, maize, potatoes and arable weed seeds are good quality food for them. They are fairly large and it is easy for them to consume a considerable amount in a short time. This reliance on agricultural foods is very important; ducks in a cereal growing area can quickly lay down good fat deposits in the autumn to tide them over the leaner winter and early spring months. Thus they enter the breeding season in good condition. For migratory 'fowl the availability of such foods helps them to overwinter successfully, ensuring their return to repopulate the northern breeding grounds in spring.

For most of the year the grazing species, principally geese, swans, wigeon and coot, require short, good quality (ie actively growing), fine, soft leaved varieties of grass on which to feed, and they will also feed on young cereal crops when available. The chances of agricultural damage are reduced if good feeding is provided close to the water which is their main day roost. These species do not like to have to travel far to graze as they like to return to their roost at intervals to drink. It is important that the grazing sites are kept free from disturbance during the day. During the summer, much of the food of these birds is taken from shallow water areas in the form of the softer leaved aquatic plants.

The simplest way to provide good grazing is to manage an area of shoreline and land around the water to maintain a short grass sward by mowing and/or grazing as necessary. Sheep produce a sward which is more attractive to grazing birds than that grazed by cattle.

The importance of invertebrate foods for breeding wildfowl

The dabbling species that rely chiefly on a granivorous or other vegetable diet in autumn and winter (and here we include wigeon) all show a marked and significant dietary switch in spring, when they become more closely "tied" to their watery breeding sites. From early spring, through the pre-laying period and right through the summer, they take almost all of their food from aquatic habitats, feeding predominantly on the larger forms of invertebrate life. Shoveler are one exception to this, in that although they will occasionally feed on flooded farmland, dabble, grub in the mud and even dive to feed, for the most part they eat chiefly larger forms of aquatic plankton, such as water fleas, which they collect by filtering large volumes of water through their fine bill lamellae.

The "macro-invertebrates" living in the open water, on and in the bed and amongst the water plants, also form the main food resource for the diving ducks, especially tufteds, goldeneye and smew, while pochard eat a little more pondweed, and the larger diving ducks (sawbills) and the grebes are fish eaters.

The birds which feed by probing in soft muds take a limited range of aquatic invertebrates, usually selecting those which occur in high densities, like midge (chironomid) larvae, oligochaete worms (*Tubifex*) and burrowing bivalve molluscs. The management of habitats to provide good conditions for feeding such birds is described in Chapter 8, in the section on water level control, and they will also benefit from the good conditions made for brood rearing as described later in this chapter.

Several studies of waterfowl breeding success have shown that food availability, principally freshwater invertebrate organisms, is a key factor in determining the density of breeding pairs and the production of fledged young.

Breeding waterfowl, especially the pre-laying females, need to consume plenty of protein, largely for egg production, and the major source of this is the invertebrate life in the water. It is known that eggs from ducks which have had a high invertebrate intake contain larger yolk reserves for the developing duckling than those from poorly fed birds. This can have an important knock-on effect for duckling survival. Also, poorly fed ducks tend to use their own body reserves to produce eggs, which reduces their mothering ability and restricts the chance of re-nesting should the first clutch be lost.

The feeding time necessary to gain the nutrients needed for the production of a clutch of eggs depends upon the abundance, quality, size and availability of the prey items. It can be deduced from this that the provision of conditions which favour the production of abundant and easily available invertebrates in the breeding area is essential if wildfowl are to breed successfully.

It should also be noted that feeding ducks need sufficient time to obtain all of their daily requirements, and so their feeding sites should be as secluded as possible.

The preferred foods of most ducks to meet their needs, as described above, in spring and early summer are freshwater shrimps, water lice, pond snails, midge, mayfly and caddis larvae, water boatmen, water fleas, beetles and worms.

Creation of good wildfowl feeding habitat

All of these creatures are found associated with beds of water plants in relatively shallow waters, where they become easily available, and

45

it is quite feasible to build the necessary habitat structure and diversity into a pond or lake, to ensure the provision of good conditions for feeding wildfowl.

The principal requirement is the creation of extensive areas of shallow water, between 5cm and 1.5m deep. This depth produces conditions which favour high biological productivity provided the plant nutrient levels are adequate. If these are limiting, the water can be enriched, as described in Chapter 8. In such shallows, the sunlight can penetrate to the bed, promoting the growth of a variety of plant life. These plants form the "scaffold" which supports and shelters many of the invertebrates, and they provide food either directly, in the form of algae and bacterial films, or indirectly as detritus when they die and decay in the water. The very shallow areas are ideal for the dabblers, probers and pickers, while the water around 1.5 to 2.5m deep is ideal for diving ducks and fish eaters.

In the construction of a new pond or lake, careful thought has to be given to the quantity and quality of spoil available, so that the best use can be made of it to make the essential shallows as well as the islands. For example, instead of spreading all available material evenly over the pond bed to make the water a uniform depth all over, it is far better to concentrate most of it in selected sites to raise the bed level, making the necessary shallow food production areas. As described earlier, it is best to retain an uneven lake bed with a wide range of depths, thus creating a variety of habitat structure underwater. This, incidentally, is also particularly important for a good fishery.

The zone of a lake which has the greatest potential for making shallow feeding sites is the shoreline. Making the shore profile as gentle as possible, eg 1 in 4 to 1 in 10, right down to the deeper water produces a very wide zone which will favour plant growth and harbour many invertebrates. The value of different shore profiles is shown in Figure 17.

Where the pond or lake is already water filled, it is possible to improve conditions by treating the edges. This usually means using a hymac type machine to cut off the upper part of the shore, regrading the profile and depositing the material in the water's edge to

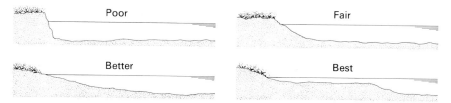

Figure 17. The correct shore profiles are important, the aim should be to create large areas of shallow water.

make the marginal shallows extend out as a sort of "wet shelf" around the pool.

The result of making graded shores and a "shelf" will be a marginal fringe of growth, with the plants in a characteristically zoned distribution as in Figure 18.

The zone progresses from the marsh plants on the landward side, through emergent and floating leaved forms, to the submerged plants of deeper water. This sort of shoreline zonation of plants becomes much compressed at gradients of 1:1 and very few will grow on shores steeper than this.

Brood rearing habitat

The plant-rich shallows made as feeding sites for breeding adult wildfowl will also be of great value later in the year as brood rearing habitat. Ducklings of almost all species are specialised insect feeders in the first couple of weeks of life, and their survival depends upon a readily available supply of hatching insects, especially midges, which are usually most abundant in the plant-rich shallows.

Further wildfowl food production areas for adults and young broods can be made by constructing shallow "scrapes" in suitably low-lying land around the outside of the main water body. It is a good plan to excavate the scrape with its bed at a slightly higher level than normal autumn water level in the lake. Water can then be pumped into the scrape as necessary to hold it full over the summer, growing the food organisms, and the scrape's water level can

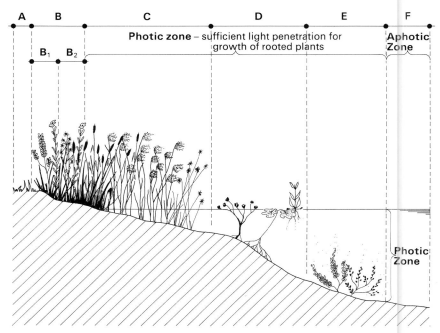

A   Terrestrial plants, soil dry in summer.
B_1 Bog plants, soil waterlogged in summer. $\Big\}$ 0-0.5 m deep
B_2 Marsh plants, soil water covered all year.
C   Reed swamp, emergent marginal vegetation: 0.5-1.5 m deep
D   Floating leaves rooted, and free floating plants: 1-3.0 m deep
E   Submerged rooted plants 1.5-11.0 m deep
F   Aphotic zone – no rooted plants in depths greater than 11.0 m
N.B. All zones overlap, depths quoted refer to clear water.

Figure 18. Water plants grow in a characteristically zoned pattern down the shore.

be lowered to expose the mud during the late summer when the broods can take advantage of the good feeding conditions. This is done quite simply by letting water flow back to the lake via the sluice channel.

Alternatively, but not quite as satisfactorily, if there is no portable (or fixed) pump available, the scrape bed can be made at a slightly lower level than the normal summer water level of the lake. This is then connected to the lake as before, ie via a channel with a simple sluice board, and water can be allowed to flow in as desired. Any

48

fall in level has to be by evaporation and seepage, and obviously such a scrape can not be completely emptied by gravity alone, so it is important to have the "humps" of an uneven bed to ensure that some mud surface is exposed when the water level is down.

The uneven bed to a scrape, with a number of high spots, some of which could be heaps of gravel to make them more stable, is highly desirable as it also means that as the water seeps away or evaporates a greater surface area becomes exposed, with more small islands appearing, and the whole thing looks more attractive than a flat sheet of uniform mud.

Many species of wader will also benefit from such habitat management. Observations made on wader use of scrapes at the Great Linford reserve indicate that, as many waders are primarily birds of estuarine habitats, they **prefer** fluctuating water levels and the associated freshly exposed mud.

Ideally, one would be able to control the water level as described above to provide a slowly receding water level and thus the necessary conditions for attracting feeding waders during their spring and autumn passage migration. A gradual fall in water level over a shore with a very gentle slope, or over a scrape with an uneven bottom, produces conditions which waders seem to find most attractive.

Shallow scrapes with the water level held constant will rapidly fill up with aquatic plants and become a marsh – which is not the desired aim, so the regular fluctuation of water levels is also valuable in that it reduces the rate of plant colonisation – in the same way that intermittent draw down of reservoirs results in bare margins. A light "sprinkling" of plants such as brooklime (*Veronica spp.*), spike rush (*Eleocharis palustris*) and perhaps bistort (*Polygonum amphibium*) is acceptable. Ducklings like the escape cover and birds such as snipe and redshank do not seem to mind a more dense plant growth. The majority of "estuary-type" waders, the dunlin, sandpipers, plovers, ruff, turnstones, etc, seem to prefer to be able to see larger expanses of open mud surface. Figure 19 shows the posision for a brood rearing and wader scrape.

A section of shore where cattle have access to drink also creates good boggy conditions for snipe and other waders. It is important,

Figure 19. Additional shallow feeding habitat can be made in "scrapes" alongside a larger pond or lake.

however, to prevent stock reaching all of the shores as they will eat down the marginal plants, and if they are allowed to enter a large part of the water body their droppings may cause localised over-enrichment.

As well as dabbling the shallows, ducklings also love to feed on insects from short grass pasture where it meets the water's edge, so some areas of the pond shore should be grazed or close mown. In addition to providing extra feeding places, these will be used by duckling broods roosting at night and will double as loafing banks and places to feed corn to the ducks in winter.

Summary – the "ideal" pond

To summarise this chapter, the ideal pond or lake basin should be varied in form. It should be as large as it can be made within the limitations of the site; be in a situation where it can be well screened

50

from disturbance; contain a variety of depths, with much of it less than 75cm deep, colonised by a wide variety of aquatic plants and invertebrates; it will have an irregular shoreline, with a range of shore profiles from very gentle slopes to vertical cliffs; there will be a number of small islands, with suitable tall, tussocky nest cover and bare areas for loafing spots; a variety of subaquatic and marginal substrates (sand, clay, topsoil, gravel, rock, etc) some areas of which must have some organic richness; and a clean, stable and reliable source of water.

CHAPTER FOUR

The Role of Water Plants in Ponds and Lakes for Wildfowl

As we have already seen from the previous chapter, the pattern of vegetation of the pond is of great importance. Basically, the water plants produce and harbour insect foods and are food in themselves for the wildfowl, while the marginal plants provide screening, cover, shelter and food. The herbaceous plants on the banks and islands provide nest cover.

The variety of wildlife species and the size of the populations supported by the new habitats is influenced mainly by the degree of variety of vegetation present because this affects the range of micro-habitats available. The potential for variety in the vegetation results from variation in the physical structure of the new water body, hence the need to achieve the correct range of physical features in the construction phase.

The establishment and control of vegetation is therefore an important part of the creation and management of a pond or lake if one is to maintain optimum conditions for waterfowl.

Establishment of aquatic plant communities

Because of the major importance of the plant communities in the ecology of a wetland, the final stages in the creation of new wildfowl habitats should be the establishment of the appropriate vegetation cover. The introduction of water plants also has the benefit of bringing in associated invertebrate life to the pond.

If a newly made lowland water body is left to colonise naturally and is allowed to develop without control, the result will be the establishment of a plant community which is dominated by only a few species, such as willows (*Salix spp.*), alder (*Alnus glutinosa*),

52

reedmace (*Typha latifolia*) and reed sweet grass (*Glyceria maxima*), with a low floral diversity. This is undesirable. It has been shown, for example, that the number of bird species using unmanaged gravel pits declines after five or six years, as these few naturally vigorous plant species become dominant.

The development of the marginal, emergent and submerged plant community, and of the terrestrial vegetation of a new site, can be greatly accelerated and diversified by the initial planting of suitable species. Such introductions determine the vegetation pattern, and thus to a large extent the fauna, of the new pond or lake for a very considerable period. It is therefore vital that the species are carefully chosen with due regard for their suitability and their intended purpose.

Planting around a pond should not be indiscriminate, but should be planned to establish a varied pattern of vegetation of native local species. The introduction of plants allows the careful positioning of the various species where they will grow well and where they will be of greatest value, for example as food producing plants, reservoirs of invertebrate life, nest cover, escape cover, shelter belts, screens, landscape features and to prevent shoreline erosion. It also ensures that the favoured species are established at an early stage as the dominant plants in the habitat.

Techniques for planting

The success rate of transplanted aquatic species is usually high and their resulting growth spread can be quite rapid. There are, however, several factors to consider when embarking on a planting programme, in particular the nature of the water body and the selection of species which suit the conditions. Is the water poor for non-aquatic plants, ie oligotrophic (nutrient-poor) and perhaps acidic, with a sand, gravel or peat substrate, or is it calcareous, alkaline, nutrient-rich and good for plant growth? Is the water cloudy or clear, deep or shallow; are the shorelines or areas to be planted suitable physically?

53

There are no commercial sources of large quantities of suitable native aquatic species, so it is necessary to locate a nearby source of appropriate transplant material at flowering time, when the various species can be identified most easily using simple field guides. This will avoid the chance of planting species which may be undesirable or already present, and the desired species can then be marked to be transplanted at the correct time.

The best way to ensure successful planting is to take material for transplanting from existing healthy stands of species which are growing well in nearby natural water bodies or slow flowing ditches. Many water plants can be obtained from nurseries and garden centres, but beware of alien or exotic species, some of which, like the Australian swamp stonecrop (*Crassula helmsii*) and water fern (*Azolla filiculoides*), are rapidly invading British freshwaters, and none of which are suited for introduction to the wild.

Material for transplanting should be collected with care, and only from situations where no damage will be done to the conservation value and where the landowner's permission is obtained.* Simply lift a section of the root or rhizome by pulling and digging with a fork. The plants are best collected just at the start of the growing season, although they can be moved at any time before they flower. The roots should be kept moist and the plants should be moved quickly to their new site and planted at once. They must not be left in heaps or in polythene sacks to "sweat"; if delay is inevitable the plants should be spread loosely in shallow water until required.

Normally little or no site preparation is needed, unless the bed is very hard rock or hard packed gravel, when a topsoil layer should be added before planting. Some books recommend the liming of acid water and fertilisation if it is nutrient-poor, but such practices are not always desirable ecologically and it would be better to restrict planting to those species known to tolerate the local conditions.

*It is essential to obtain the landowner's permission before collecting any plant material. Several water plants are rare or endangered species, given special protection, and these must not be disturbed. If in doubt, it is wise to consult your English Nature, Scottish Natural Heritage or Countryside Council for Wales Regional Officer.

The planting techniques are very simple. For emergent marginal plants, any excess top growth is cut off and the root (rhizome) is pushed into soft soil just on the waterline; in heavy clay or gravelly soils it will first be necessary to use a spade to cut a small slot into which the roots can be pressed. The material is then carefully firmed in by hand or foot. One species, *Phragmites australis*, the common reed, has proved notoriously difficult to establish unless it is planted in damp soil rather than in the water. If a long slit trench is made, parallel to the waterline, about 20cm up the shore, a bundle of freshly lifted young, green reed stems, attached to a section of rhizome, can be laid down in the trench and covered with soil to leave about 20cms of the tips exposed. These will then sprout new vertical shoots from each node, resulting in rapid establishment. Once growing, the reed bed will extend down the shore.

Submerged and floating leaved species must be planted in a similar depth to that from which they were collected, up to 40cm deep for convenience. These can be either rooted plants or, for many of the submerged species, simply cuttings pushed into the mud. In deeper water, cuttings or rooted plants can be pushed into clay balls, which are then dropped overboard from a boat. The leafy tips of many of the submerged species will grow if simply thrown into the water, but the success is not great and there is no control over where they become established. Some of the useful wildfowl food plants such as arrowhead, broad-leaved and sago pondweed (fennel-leaved pondweed) produce tubers or overwintering buds called turions, and these can be collected in autumn for broadcasting into the water, or they can be stuck into clay balls and sunk. Very shallow areas, where there is just a centimetre or two of water, or even just wet soil, should be planted with marsh or fen species, such as kingcup, brooklime, spike-rush, mares-tail, water forget-me-not, arrowhead, great water dock or gipsy-wort, which are good for duckling and wader cover, using whole rooted plants.

In any aquatic planting scheme only a small number of each species needs to be introduced; most of them spread quite rapidly and once established they can be moved and transplanted within the pond to fill in any gaps.

The success rate for rooted and rhizomatous species is greatest if the planting is done in spring, just as the new shoots appear at the end of the plant's dormant period, and it should always be done before flowering. After flower production, the growth of most water plants slows down, and while autumn planting does work, it is usually less successful and plants may wash out over winter. If autumn planting is unavoidable, the plants may need to be held in place by a wire peg or weighted down with stones.

Whenever the plants are introduced, if there is a coot, swan or goose population they will soon be removed and so they must be protected with a cover of wire mesh until firmly rooted. Similarly, plantings on exposed shores will need the protection of a floating pole wave baffle to reduce the effects of wave action (Figure 20).

The most productive zone of the lake is often the interface or "edge" between two different stands of vegetation or between the

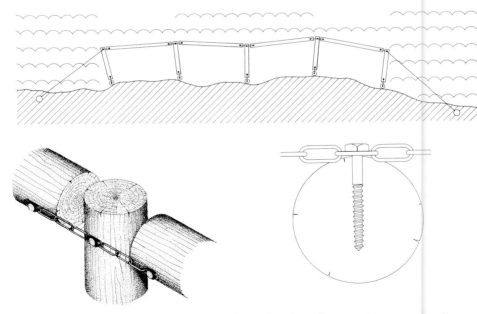

Figure 20. A wave baffle of floating telegraph poles or logs must be very soundly constructed.

vegetation and open water. Here, water and nutrients can circulate freely, light can penetrate and invertebrates have easy access, as also do fish and ducks. It is desirable to create as much "edge" as possible during planting.

The rhizomatous, emergent species normally grow in mono-cultures, forming pure stands, and several small blocks of different species along a shore are much preferred to a few very large stands of any one species. These plants should therefore be introduced in single species blocks along the shores, and each block should be of sufficient length to ensure that it becomes firmly established before meeting competition from a neighbouring, perhaps more vigorous, one. These single species blocks should also be in a varied pattern along the shore to increase the diversity of habitats.

Wherever possible, planting should be planned so that the final effect is the reproduction of a natural pattern of plant zones as far down the shore as possible, extending from the marginal marsh plants on the land down to submerged species offshore, as illustrated in Figure 18. This is not only more stable and more productive than haphazard planting, but it is much more pleasing aesthetically.

If very vigorous, potentially invasive plants, such as common reed, reedmace and worst of all reed sweet grass, are introduced, their spread can be limited if they are only planted where their growth will be restricted by local conditions, eg on a ridge sur-

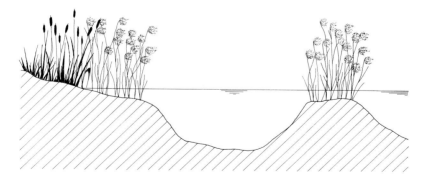

Figure 21. The spread of invasive species of emergent plants can be restricted by confining them to areas surrounded by deep water.

rounded by deep water (over 2.0m) or on the marginal shelf of a steep shore (Figure 21).

Reedmace *(Typha latifolia)* may overcome this depth limitation by growing out over the water as a floating mass of dense, tangled rhizomes. This should be watched for, and prevented if the water area is not to be diminished.

Plant species suitable for introduction

Table 1 Plant species suitable for wildfowl habitats

Shoreline Zone as in Fig. 18

Plant Species	A	B₁	B₂	C	D	E
Alders	●	●				
Great willowherb	●	●				
Forget-me-not	●	●				
Woundwort	○	●				
Gipyswort	○	●	○			
Marsh marigold	○	●	○			
Sweet flag		○	●	○		
Flowering rush		○	●	○		
Spike rush		○	●	○		
Water plantain		○	●	●		
Jointed rush		●	●			
Willows	●	●	○			
Bur-marigold	●	●	○			
Sea club-rush		○	●	●		
Reedmace		○	●	●		
Brooklime		●	●	○		
Water cress		●	●	○		
Water mint		●	●	○		
Great water dock		●	●	●		
Marestail		●	●	●		
Meadowsweet	●	●	○			
Hard rush	○	●	●			
Soft rush	○	●	●			

Table 1 – continued

Plant Species	A	B₁	B₂	C	D	E
Reed canary grass	○	●	●	○		
Bog bean	○	●	●	○		
Marsh horsetail	○	●	●	○		
Pond sedges	○	●	●	○		
Purple-loosestrife	○	●	●	○		
Yellow iris	○	●	●	○		
Great yellow cress	○	●	●	○		
Bur-reed	○	●	●	●		
Reed grass	○	●	●	●		
Common reed	○	●	●	●		
Bulrush			○	●		
Arrowhead		●	○	○		
Duckweed			●	●	●	●
Amphibious bistort	●	●	●	●	●	
Water lilies			○	●	●	
Quillwort			○	●	●	●
Water crowfoot			○	○	●	●
Water lobelia			○	●	●	●
Broad-leaved pondweed			○	○	●	●
Water parsnip			○	○	●	●
Lesser water parsnip			○	○	●	●
Bladderwort			○	○	●	●
Water soldier			○	○	●	●
Frogbit			○	○	●	○
Hornwort			○	○	●	●
Canadian pondweed			○	○	●	●
Spiked milfoil			○	○	●	●
Whorled milfoil			○	○	●	●
Stonewort				○	○	●

Key

● species characteristically found in this zone   ○ species sometimes found in this zone

The value of various plant species for wildfowl

Table 2 The value of aquatic plants to wildfowl

Species	Growth Habit	Value	Uses
Watercrowsfoot	Submerged	E	IS(V)
Tassel pondweed (Wigeon grass)	Submerged	U	VSI
Stonewort	Submerged	G	SI
Canadian pondweed	Submerged	E	I(V)
Milfoil	Submerged	E	I(V)
Horned pondweed	Submerged	VG	IS
Fennel-leaved pondwood (Sago pondwood)	Submerged	VG	IS
Hornwort	Submerged	U	I
Starwort	Submerged and floating leaved	VG	I(V)
Duckweeds	Free-floating	VG	V
Broad-leaved pondweed	Floating leaved	G	SI
*Amphibious bistort	Floating leaved	VG	ISB
*Water lilies	Floating leaved	G	IB
Arrowhead	Emergent in shallows	E	IVB
*Marestail	Emergent in shallows	VG	ISB
*Bur-reed	Emergent in shallows and on wet soils	VG	IS(N)
Spike rush	Emergent in shallows	VG	SIB
Sea club-rush	Emergent in shallows	E	SIBW(N)
Sedges	Emergent in shallows and on wet soils	VG	ISN
Yellow iris	Emergent in shallows and on wet soils	U	I(N)
*Common (Norfolk) reed	Emergent in moderate depth, to damp soils	U	W(N)(I)
Bulrush	Emergent from moderate depth	G	IS(N)

Table 2 – continued

Species	Growth Habit	Value	Uses
*Reedmace	Emergent from moderate depth to wet soils	U	IW(N)
Rushes	Wet to damp soils	G	N
Brambles, nettles, thistles, willowherb, purple-loosestrife, tufted hair-grass		E	N

*These species can cause problems by choking very shallow water, reducing its value to wildfowl.

Key

Value		Uses	
		I – Harbours invertebrates as food	B – Attractive to broods
E – Excellent	G – Good	S – Seeds readily eaten	N – Used for nesting
VG – Very Good	U – Useful	V – Vegetation eaten	W – Provides winter cover
			( ) Limited use

Once the vegetation communities are successfully established, attention in future years will be directed more towards the management of plants in and around the water to maintain optimum conditions, as described in detail in Chapter 8.

CHAPTER FIVE

Planning and Legal Aspects, and Grant Aid for New Waters

If you are planning to make a pond or lake it will be necessary to first consider the legal and planning requirements as these can determine what may or may not be feasible. It is extremely difficult to cover in one short chapter such a very complex and frequently changing subject as the planning and legal requirements relating to pond and lake construction. The different licensing regulations change with time and are often interpreted in different ways by each National Rivers Authority region. This makes it impossible to give precise information which will be accurate for the whole country.

This chapter can therefore only provide general guidelines to illustrate the various aspects of legislation relating to the construction of ponds and lakes. This makes it essential to discuss any pond or lake construction project with all of the interested parties mentioned below, in particular the regional unit of the NRA, well before any work is started.

Planning consent

Provided that the work is entirely "within the holding", the construction of *small* farm ponds and lakes for conservation, landscape and agricultural purposes may not require planning consent from your County, District or Borough Council. Such activities are often considered to be permitted agricultural development. Even so, this is known to be a "grey area" in planning control and it is advisable to hold informal discussions of the proposals with the local Planning Authority.

In cases where the construction work is not confined to the holding and involves the transport of excavated material or infill onto or off the site via the public highway, the County Planning Office must be consulted for their views. Where the lake is to be made by the removal of sand and gravel for sale it will be essential to make a fully detailed planning application to obtain consent for mineral extraction from the County Council, and detailed excavation and restoration plans must be submitted for approval. The Local Authority and NRA are empowered to impose conditions on such excavations. For more details see Chapter 7, on the restoration of gravel pits for wildfowl.

Also, if you are considering the creation of a large new lake, pond or reservoir which will have a major effect on the landscape or drainage, you may need planning consent for a change of land use, so as a first step it is worth discussing your plans informally with the Planning Officer of your County Council. This is particularly important if you live within a designated Area of Outstanding Natural Beauty (AONB) or one of the recently declared Environmentally Sensitive Areas (ESAs), in which case the local MAFF Officer must be consulted. If you live within a National Park it would also be necessary to consult the National Park Authority before starting work on any form of pond or lake.

Regional Water Authorities and licensing

Prospective pond builders should also be aware that the type of water body that is intended will determine whether or not you need permission and licensing from the NRA or Internal Drainage Board. "Off-stream" ponds and lakes, cut off from flowing water (except rainfall and surface run-off) so that water can only enter under control, eg via a sluice, through a pipe with a valve or by being pumped from a source of standing surface water (not an underground aquifer) are not regulated by the NRA. However, an abstraction licence will be required from the relevant Authority for the initial filling of such a pond, unless it is solely for agricultural purposes other than spray irrigation (for example to rear food fish not used for sport). If it is used for any other purpose, including recreation, the filling will need to be licensed and paid for. "Off-stream" ponds which are dug below the level of the water table and are filled and fed only by groundwater seepage do not need licensing unless the water is to be pumped out of them, in which case a licence to abstract water will be necessary.

The situation with regard to "on-stream" water bodies, where water enters via a stream with no control, is complex and depends partly on how they are made. If there are any works made in a water course that alter the flow or retain water above the original ground level, the project will automatically come under NRA jurisdiction under the terms of the Water Resources Act (1963) and the Water Act of 1973. Such projects will probably require a licence issued under the Water Resources Act (1963). The NRA will also regulate the work to ensure that it meets the conditions laid down in the licence. Their engineering staff are fully experienced in such things as weir, sluice, dam and spillway design, and will give informal advice on site, but for all but the smallest schemes it is advisable to obtain professional advice on the details of design and construction.

If the pond is made so that it raises the water level above that of the water table in the surrounding land, then a licence to impound water will be required from your local NRA office. This will take into account any alterations to the flow of the feeder stream which may affect its use by the upstream and downstream Riparian Owners, in that their water supply, quality and/or land drainage may be affected. This being so, it would be advisable to discuss significant proposals with neighbours so as to avoid any possibility of later conflict.

It is normally acceptable if the surplus water from your pond flows into a water course, unless there is a marked change in water quality – as would be the case if the pond was used for intensive fish rearing, in which case a consent under the Control of Pollution Act to discharge to the water course will be necessary. Your local National Rivers Authority Unit will be pleased to advise on such matters, and in any case it would again be wise to consult them at an early stage.

In most pond or lake building projects, and particularly where the impoundment volume is large or the structures required are substantial, the NRA will require detailed plans to be submitted for their approval before any work may commence, and the appropriate notices will need to be published. Their concern will only be over the details of the necessary licensing however. Their approval will not relate to the safety of any structural works; these are a matter for the pond owner and his advisors. If the pond or lake is to be made within a river flood plain, the NRA will need to give their approval to the plans for spoil disposal, their concern normally being about the adverse effects of any alteration in ground level on the floodwater flow. In practice, there is a general prohibition on the erection of banks in a flood plain so any surplus spoil from an excavation will probably have to be removed from the site.

Dams made to impound water in stream valleys must be constructed with great care and it is essential to seek professional advice from a chartered engineer before proceeding with anything but the smallest earth dam. If the dam impounds a water volume greater than 22 500 cubic metres (5 million gallons) above the level of the surrounding ground – that is more than 1ha at an average depth of 2.25m (= 3 acres more than 6 feet deep) – then, in accordance with the Reservoirs Act (1975) it must be designed by a specially qualified engineer (ie a civil engineer who has been appointed by the Secretary of State for the Environment to Panel 1 of the Reservoirs Inspectors Panel), and this is likely to be costly. The design of simple earth dams is covered in the section on construction in Chapter 6. Advice on the relevant detail of the Reservoirs Act (1975) can be obtained from the County Council in whose area the lake is to be built.

Government bodies and SSSIs

If the proposed site is part of a scheduled Site of Special Scientific Interest or one of the recently designated "Special Protection Areas" (SPAs), it is a mandatory legal requirement to consult the Regional Officer of English Nature, Scottish Natural Heritage or the

Countryside Council for Wales before commencing any work on a new pond or lake. This will automatically be done by the National Rivers Authority Unit when they are made aware of the scheme, but even if the project is outside their field of interest, and is not in an SSSI, it would be wise to consult the EN Regional Officer; his advice might prevent you from flooding an area which is already very valuable ecologically.

Availability of grant aid

As the great landscape garden designers of the past showed so well, almost any water body will, if designed and sited in such a way that it appears to be natural, become an attractive focal point, enhancing the landscape. This being the case, it would be worth approaching the Countryside Commission, either directly or via your County Council, as there may be a possibility of discretionary grant aid of up to 50% of the total cost. A similar discretionary grant may be available from EN if the pond is to be primarily for wildlife conservation.

If its main purpose is agricultural, eg for an irrigation scheme, for stock watering, or as part of a farm diversification scheme (and this includes conservation, recreation and sporting use) then it may be grant aided by up to 30% by the Ministry of Agriculture; their Regional Office will be able to provide details. In addition to the above, some National Park Authorities may give grant aid and some Local Authorities may give aid for the restoration of neglected waters.

Each application is considered on its merits. If your scheme does qualify for a grant, there will almost certainly be specific conditions to be met and if you do wish to apply for such grants, only one source can be accepted for each project, and you *must* have the grant details confirmed before any construction work begins.

*We are very grateful to Mr E Parson of the Anglian Water Authority's NRA Unit at Chelmsford and Mr W Fowler of the Anglian Water Authority's Water Resources Department for their valuable help and advice on this chapter.

CHAPTER SIX

The Siting and Construction of Ponds and Lakes

The chapter on legal and planning aspects pointed out the need to consult with the relevant authorities before starting work on all but the smallest pond building projects. This chapter describes the methods of construction that can be used to make ponds and lakes, and gives details of various water level control and flood relief structures. This should help the reader to decide on which method should be used, and to draw up the plans for a modest scheme. We must, however, reiterate the need to seek specialist advice from a qualified chartered engineer for more ambitious projects, and again it would be wise to consult the Regional Office of NRA at an early stage.

Where should the pond or lake be?

The first consideration in a pond building project is to identify a suitable site. The position chosen will depend primarily upon the topography, the potential catchment area and water supply, the groundwater table and the soil type. Where possible it should be in a quiet secluded part of the farm, away from roads, paths, houses, sources of potential pollution and overhead power lines. If it can be sited on an existing wildfowl flight line, so much the better. It is important to try to link it in with the overall conservation plan for the farm, siting it so that it is not totally isolated, but is linked to the other habitats, eg hedgerows, woodland and meadows.

Choice of construction method

Ponds may be made in a number of ways. The method selected for any particular site will depend upon the topography, soil conditions and drainage characteristics of the area. It will also, of course, be influencd by the possible cost.

Seepage filled excavations

Digging a suitably shaped basin in permeable soils where the water table is close to the surface, allowing it to fill from groundwater seepage as in Figure 22, may be the most cost-effective method, especially if there is gravel present, in which case it may be possible to obtain planning consent to extract this to pay for the work.

Run-off filled excavations

In areas where the soil contains a high proportion of clay, ie around 15–30%, making it relatively impervious, scraping out a depression in a valley floor, as in Figure 23, and relying on run-off and drainage from the surrounding catchment area can be effective.

With an annual rainfall of 50cm, a run-off fed pond of 0.4ha with an average depth of 60cm would need a catchment of, at the very least, 8.0ha – more if the soils were very permeable – so such ponds are best made in the wetter north-west of the country. Unfortunately, such run-off fed ponds and those fed by groundwater seepage will probably suffer from a seasonal change in water level of up

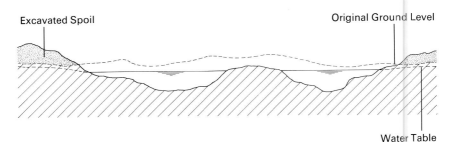

Figure 22. Excavating below the water table in permeable soils is a simple way to make a pond.

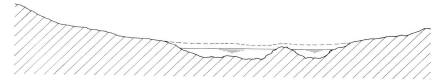
Figure 23. A pond may be made by deepening a natural depression on a valley floor, so that it collects surface water run-off.

to 0.5m. This seasonal water level fluctuation will be lessened if the pond is made where it can be supplied with water from a reliable spring.

The use of membrane liners

On permeable soils with the water table some way below ground level, eg on sands or chalk, the only way such a pond could be guaranteed to hold water would be to use a puddled clay, 1000 gauge polythene, PVC or butyl liner.

Though expensive to buy, such liners may still be cheaper than the costs of major excavations and dam construction, and so are worth investigating. Their main disadvantages are that they are vulnerable to damage, especially if they become exposed when they may also degrade due to the effects of ultra violet light, they are not particularly easy to lay over large areas as the sheets will need to be joined on site, and sites must be carefully prepared (ie cleared of sharp objects) before laying.

Polythene sheet (1000g) is usually the cheapest material, and black lasts longer than clear sheet if it is exposed to light, but if it is covered with 15–20cm of soil it should be very long lasting. This need for soil cover does mean that it is not suitable for use on steep slopes, where the soil would slide off into deeper water.

Butyl rubber is the most expensive material and, if chosen, it should be 30/1000s inch thick. This material is much stronger and more flexible than polythene and therefore easier to lay, less prone to damage and very long lasting. It should still, however, be covered with soil.

The most frequently used pond liner is 14/1000 inch grade PVC sheeting; it is much better than polythene, being stronger, more flexible and with a longer life, even if exposed to sunlight.

The laying of sheet liners requires good site preparation, but is not difficult. Newly formed banks should be firmly consolidated and the slope of the shore should be no more than 1 in 3, otherwise the soil covering will slide off. If laid with some slack, ie with a few small folds, the sheet will mould itself to gentle contours but not sharp angles, and so any large stones must be removed, with the resulting holes being filled in. If the ground is at all stony, especially if there are many exposed flints, the area to be covered by the sheet should be screeded with a 10–15cm layer of sand or stone-free earth before laying the sheet.

The sheet must be adequately large to cover the area, with spare material to allow for the irregularities of the bed and to be buried at the edges in order to anchor it in place. The edge of the sheet should be taken down the side of the surrounding edge trench and across its base before the trench is filled and tamped to anchor the sheet in place on the shore (Figure 24a).

With PVC and polythene sheet any surplus material can be folded over to form pleats where necessary to try to lay the sheet without wrinkles. In fact it is important not to stretch the sheet taut when anchoring it, otherwise the weight of water on it when filled will press it down into all of the minor hollows, perhaps causing it to

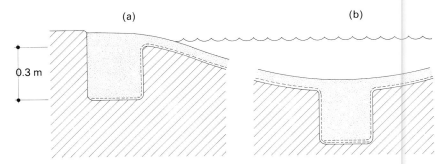

(a)   (b)

0.3 m

Figures 24a, 24b. The edge and joins in a pond liner need to be securely anchored in a trench.

tear. Butyl rubber on the other hand should not be folded into creases and any surplus should be taken to the edge and buried in the anchoring trench, which may need to be deepened accordingly. Butyl sheet is more elastic than the other materials and will thus mould itself a little better to bed irregularities. It must not, however, be pulled tight during the laying process.

Joining sheet liners may be necessary as their width is limited, and this can be done on site, with the edges overlapped and buried in a specially dug trench, as in Figure 24b. The joins should be arranged so that they run up and down, not across, the slope of the banks, so that they are under less lateral strain. Polythene and PVC sheet may be joined by overlapping adjacent sheets by 150mm and sealing the overlapped strip with mastic sealant before covering the joint edge with a strip of 75mm wide waterproof adhesive tape. The sheets must, of course, be dry for this operation.

Once laid, the sheet liner must be covered with a minimum of 15cm of stone-free soil or sand, and this is only possible on slopes of less than 1:3, which is a good gradient for the shores of a wildfowl water. On a steeper shore the sheet margin should be anchored as shown in Figure 25.

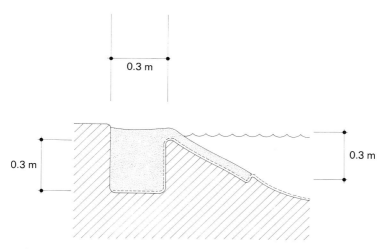

Figure 25. On a steeper shore, the edge of the liner should be covered like this.

Excavated stream bed pools

Excavating a pool into the bed of a stream, with an increase in surface area but no change in water level, is a very simple way of making a pond on a level valley floor, and this is shown in Figure 26.

Disposal of spoil from excavations

The excavation of a pond or lake will inevitably produce a large volume of spoil to dispose of and this can be a problem. The amount of spoil to be generated can easily be calculated and the question of its disposal can be a major factor in the design of a new pond or lake. This should therefore be given a high priority at the planning

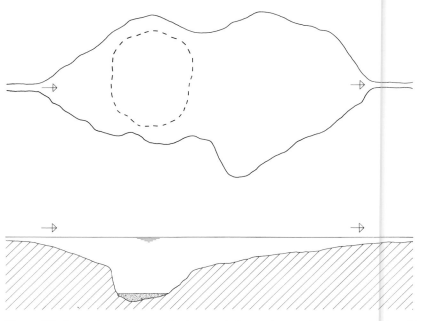

Figure 26. A pool made by widening and deepening a stream course should have a deeper section upstream to slow down flow and to act as a silt trap.

stage. Ideally, the excavated material should not have to be transported far, as this involves heavy costs. If possible it should be used around the pond, to raise a small screening embankment, well back from the water's edge, so that it may be planted with suitable trees and shrubs without them adversely affecting the water or its use as a flight pond or fishery. If the water is to be used as a flight pond it is a good plan to leave spaces in the embankment to build the hides. If, however, your new pond is dug in the flood plain of a river, it is most unlikely that the NRA would approve of it being used to raise the land level around the pond, as this could interfere with floodwater flow.

In other circumstances the deposition of earth mounds might well adversely affect the quality of the landscape, or spoil someone's previously uninterrupted view. The site for the pond has thus to be chosen partly with spoil disposal in mind.

Where the new water is being made by a combination of excavation and damming of a stream, the spoil will obviously be used for the dam and possibly to create a wall to divert the stream flow past the dam site during construction, but in these cases it must contain at least 15% clay, and be cohesive and compactable. Details of this are given later in this chapter.

Use of spoil for landfill

If the above is not feasible, it might be possible to put the spoil to good use elsewhere on the farm, for example to fill in any hollows, or to raise the soil level in any poorly drained wet areas, bearing in mind, of course, that this may not be desirable if such wet spots are already valuable botanical conservation features, as they often are.

If spoil is to be disposed of to raise the level of land in cultivation, the operation must be done with great care. If possible the topsoil should be stripped from the excavation site and stored in a low heap, less than 1m high, to retain it in good condition. The underlying land should then be ripped with a subsoiler and the material from the excavation should be tipped at the infill site, being placed and spread in position with a low ground pressure hymac type machine, working from the original ground level, so as not to compact the material being placed. Figure 27 shows the details of the infilling process.

When a band of spoil equal to the reach of the machine has been placed in position it should be covered with 15-20cm of topsoil in the same way. The filling of the low spots thus continues in a series of bands, so that the machine **never actually runs on the surface of the infill**. The filled area should be left with a slightly domed surface profile; this leaves the area to settle naturally, without compaction forming a panned layer. Once settled the new surface should be seeded with grass, again using low ground pressure vehicles.

It should be borne in mind, of course, that some of the excavated material may be needed on site to complete the construction of islands and the correct profiling of the shorelines, if necessary using some to make very shallow marsh areas extending out into the main water body, but this does rely on an accurate prediction of the final water level.

Damming a stream to make a pool

Building a dam across a stream to hold back the water in a valley is an obvious choice of construction method, making a pond as shown in Figure 28. This method usually provides the greatest pond area and stored volume at the lowest cost. It is, however, the most complex method in terms of design and construction detail.

Such on-stream ponds must have a correctly designed dam to hold back the water. They must also incorporate a level control device to take normal water flows and, to prevent washout, an overspill weir capable of taking the maximum flood flow. If possible, facilities for complete draw down should also be included in the design, especially if the pond is to be used as a fishery.

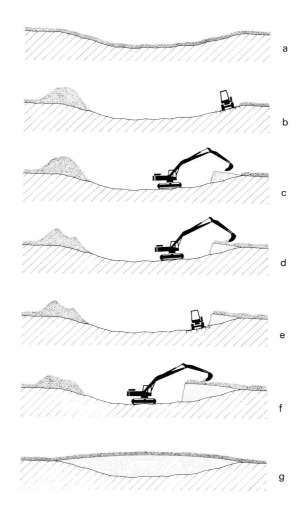

Figures 27a–27g. Disposal of excavated spoil to raise land levels.
a – The low area to be filled.
b – The topsoil stripped and stored, the subsoil ripped.
c – The spoil from the pond is placed on the ripped subsoil strip.
d – The topsoil is placed on top of the infilled strip.
e – The next section of the subsoil is ripped.
f – The next strip of infil and topsoil placed in position.
g – The completed infilling with a domed profile to allow for settlement.

75

Figure 28. On-stream ponds should have a silt trap at the point of water inlet.

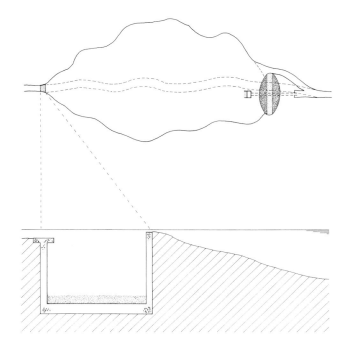

Figure 29. Detail of the silt trap chamber.

On-stream ponds

Dams which create on-stream ponds obviously have to be capable of holding back the entire volume of water which is raised above the level of the base of the dam and they must be able to cope with the *maximum flood flow of the whole upstream catchment*. On-stream ponds are therefore generally unsuitable where the catchment exceeds 200ha as the flood overspill structure necessary to cope with storm run-off from such an area has to be very complex. Further, it must be remembered that any dam higher than 4.5m or which retains more than 5 million gallons of water above the original

76

ground must be designed by a Chartered Engineer appointed by the Secretary of State for the Environment to the Reservoirs Inspectors Panel. These requirements can make large dams costly to build.

Also, the shape of the water body made by damming a stream depends upon the height of the overflow at the dam and the upstream profile of the valley, and so it is not therefore easy to modify.

The gradient of the valley is important, too. In a steep valley the stream below the dam can erode back unless the toe of the dam is protected, eventually undercutting the dam and causing it to fail. In all cases, unless very carefully designed and built, using correct quality materials on fully suitable sites, it is possible that the dam may settle, slip, seep or leak underneath and either dam face may erode in flood times. An important point to bear in mind is that an outlet capable of carrying normal stream and flood flow will be necessary in the base of the dam during the construction phase, unless the whole stream is diverted along the valley side in a new channel of adequate dimensions, rejoining the original stream some way below the dam site.

Details of dam, level control and flood spillway design and construction are given later in this chapter.

On-stream ponds above dams suffer from another important disadvantage in that when the stream water enters, the flow rate falls suddenly and the suspended solids in the water will settle out. Over a long period this silt will accumulate and gradually fill the pond, and many existing on-stream ponds are seen which have suffered badly from many years of silting. Where practical, this should be removed by dredging and in some cases further silt deposition may be prevented by re-routing the feeder stream in a new channel around the pond.

In new on-stream ponds a wide, deep silt trap chamber (with a wide outlet to make the outflow water shallow and thus to slow the flow rate) should be built at the point of entry of the stream. The sudden decrease in flow rate as the stream enters the chamber will cause the suspended solids to fall out of suspension and the collected silt can then be removed as necessary (Figure 29).

Off-stream ponds

For the above reasons it is much better if the pond is made "off-stream", ie excavated or made with raised banks or a dam *alongside*, rather than right on the stream course. This removes or reduces most of the above problems (Figure 30).

In floods the excess water and its silt load will by-pass the pond so a smaller spillway or outlet is needed (if any), and there will be less silting. There will be less change to the character of the stream above and below the pond, less erosion at the inlet and outlet, easier control over water level (a very important point) and the pond basin and dam can be constructed in dry conditions without the need for a stream by-pass channel, giving better opportunities to create ideal conditions (shallows, peninsulas, islands etc.) before the water is allowed in.

Very small off-stream ponds where the water lies mainly below the level of the surrounding land, or simply fills a natural depression, require no outlet structures. Once filled, the inlet merely compensates for water loss by seepage and evaporation.

However, if the off-stream pond is made by raising a dam or any

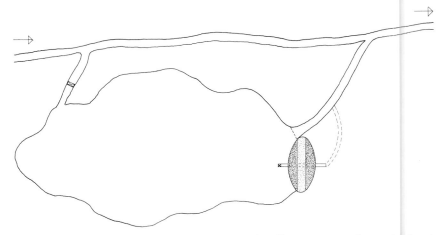

Figure 30. An off-stream pond does not need a silt trap or complex water level control and flood overspill structures.

form of embankment to hold back the water, or if the stream is subject to severe flooding, the inlet needs more careful consideration and some form of outlet pipe or channel from the pond will be required.

The inlet to such off-stream ponds must be smaller in size (usually a small diameter pipe) than any outlet pipe or channel so that the pond will not overflow its banks. The maximum level of water in such a pond will then be determined by the diameter of the outlet pipe as this will not flow at its full rate until the head of water above its mouth is 1.2 times its diameter. Thus, if the inflow rate should increase, a pond with a 15cm outlet would show a rise in water level of 18cm above the mouth of the outlet pipe.

The end of the inlet pipe should be raised clear of the stream bed, but with the invert below minimum dry weather stream flow and protected by a mesh screen. The end of the inlet should also be arranged so that it angles back in a downstream direction. As well as reducing the amount of silt carried into the pipe, this means that inflow rate decreases as the stream velocity increases in flood times, reducing the risk of the pond bursting its banks. It is a good idea to incorporate a gate valve or sluice in the inlet to enable inflow to be regulated (see Figure 31).

Selection of sites for earth dams

The first step in impounding water to make a pool by a dam on a stream is to select a suitable site. This should be where the smallest dam will retain the largest surface area, but not necessarily the largest volume of water. The sort of place to look for is therefore a narrowing of the stream valley below a fairly level, wide, shallow basin in the valley floor. Avoid siting the dam where rock outcrops occur in the valley walls as this makes it very difficult to key in the ends of the dam.

It should also be ensured that the stream flow will be adequate to maintain the water level in the pool. Very small streams should not be dammed as the evaporation loss from an exposed, shallow

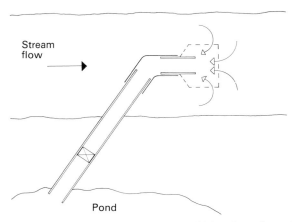

Figure 31. The inlet to an off-stream pond should be via a pipe with its mouth opening away from the direction of stream flow and with a control valve on the pipe.

pool in midsummer can be as much as 6mm per day, equal to 4.0 litres per hectare per minute. If, therefore, your proposed pond covers 2ha, and minimum dry weather flow in the stream drops below 8.0 litres per minute, not only will the water level fall, but the stream below the pond will dry up. In such cases it is best to make only a very small pond, or seek another site.

Testing the suitability of the soil

The subsoil on the site must be suitable for an earth dam. If when freshly dug you can roll it into a thin sausage shape between your palms, without it breaking up (after discarding any pebbles), it is probably usable. When moistened and rubbed between your fingers it should feel smooth and slippery, but also slightly gritty.

A good way to test the suitability of the soil is to shake up thoroughly a handful of the soil in a jar of water so that all lumps are broken up, then allow the contents to settle until the water is clear. The various component particle sizes will then be visible as layers in the bottom of the jar and the proportions of each can be estimated (Figure 32).

80

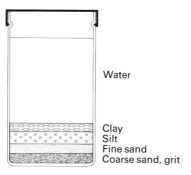

Figure 32. Allowing the soil sample to settle out after shaking in a water-filled jar is a simple way to determine the composition of the soil and its suitability for dam building.

What you need is a minimum clay fraction of between 10% and 25%, with less than 30% silt (silt particles being slightly coarser than clay), with a total silt plus clay content of around 50%. The remainder of the soil will be made up of coarser sand, grit and gravel sized particles. The test should be done on soil from a number of test holes dug a cross the line of the dam and if the soil on site contains less than 10% clay it will be essential to build the dam with a core of high clay-content soil.

The types of soil most suitable are good heavy clays, clay loams, silty clay loams and hoggin (gravel, sand and clay) down to the bedrock. Pure clay is adequate for building dam cores but if used for the entire dam, will suffer badly from cracking as the outer, downstream face dries out.

Details of the construction technique for earth dams with and without clay cores are given later in this chapter. The following general points and details of outlet and overspill structures apply to both types.

Diversion of stream flow

It is very important to consider where the stream flow will go during dam construction. It will be a rare case where the dam could be built to keep up with the rising water level, and in any event, this is undesirable as the stream would be dried up downstream until the overflow was working.

There are normally two alternatives. One is to pipe the stream for the section which flows through the dam site, as in Figure 33. The other way is to divert it in a new channel along the valley side, around the end of the proposed dam, to join the original course some way below the dam as in Figure 34.

Re-routing under the dam site

This option is normally chosen where stream flow is low enough to be taken by a pipe of a suitable dimension, and where the dam can be built in mid to late summer, with a low possibility of flash floods occurring. The plastic or concrete pipe should be chosen so that it runs less than 25% full at normal stream flow rate, with a

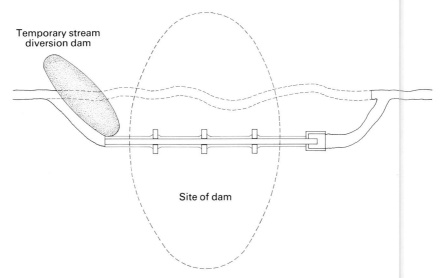

Figure 33. Diversion of the stream flow under the site of the dam by means of a pipe allows the dam to be made in dry conditions.

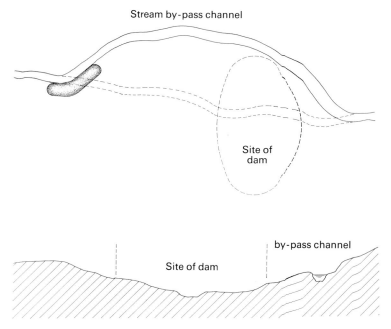

Figure 34. Re-routing the stream in a by-pass channel is an alternative to the under-dam pipe.

minimum size of 15cm diameter. This pipe should be set into a new trench dug alongside the stream bed into the subsoil underneath the base of the proposed dam, with a very gradual fall (1:100 being sufficient) and it is important at this point to ensure that the invert of the upstream end of the pipe is set at the lowest level to which you wish to draw down the water. The pipe must be buried to a depth of at least twice its own diameter.

The trench should be carefully backfilled with clay soil, compacting it in 15cm layers, making sure that it is packed under the pipe too. If the dam has to be built with a clay core, the trench for the pipe should be dug after the first part of the clay core has been made in the soil under the dam base. It will thus pass through the section of the core which lies below original ground level, not through the new earth dam. The section of dam core cut by the pipe trench should be backfilled with clay, with a concrete anti-seepage collar about 1m along on the upstream run of the pipe.

These anti-seepage collars are required along the pipe at intervals of 10 × pipe diameter to stop water flow along the outside of the pipe. If neglected, this seepage could gradually increase and result in washout by undermining the dam foundations. To build one of these, a short cross trench should be dug at right angles to the pipe and deeper than the main trench, about 5 × pipe diameter from side to side and top to bottom. This should be left clear when filling the main trench with clay soil. When the main trench is filled, the cross trenches must be filled with a lean concrete mix and well tamped around the pipe to form a concrete collar around it. The details are shown in Figure 35.

When building the dam, the section of pipe under the dam must not be tracked over by earthmoving machinery until at least 1m of clay soil has been packed firmly but carefully over it, otherwise it may move or crack, causing a potential site for future dam failure.

Re-routing around the dam site

If the stream flow is too great to be taken by a pipe of a convenient diameter, it must be diverted past the dam site in a newly made channel. This by-pass channel has to be dug along the side wall of the valley, with as gentle a gradient as possible, to lead the stream well clear of the end of the dam and back into the original stream bed further downstream (Figure 34). This is not really very practical on steep valley sites, as the diverted stream would have to rejoin the main flow at a steep angle, necessitating the construction of a substantial chute to prevent erosion which, in time, could cut back to the foot of the dam, causing it to fail.

The stream is diverted into the new channel by means of a temporary dam while the main dam site is cleared. The dam and associated water level control and flood overspill structures may then be built in the dry. Even in projects which rely on the by-pass channel, it is advisable to build in an under-dam drainage pipe as above, com-

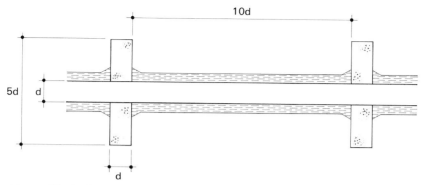

Figure 35. A pipe laid under an earth dam should have concrete anti-seepage collars along it.

plete with a valve to close it off, or with a monk sluice outlet (see below). This can then drain away any rainwater or seepage during dam building, and can be used to drain the pool when necessary.

If the dam is to be built in the autumn, winter or spring it will be essential to ensure that the by-pass channel is able to accept the total flood flow of the stream, otherwise the working area may flood, with potentially disastrous results – your half completed dam may disappear!

When the dam is completed, has settled and is grassed over, the original stream channel can be re-opened to fill the dam. If possible, the by-pass channel should remain as an emergency flood spillway.

However, if the stream by-pass channel can be made large enough, on a gentle gradient, dug into good clay-rich soil or lined with stone cladding, gabions or concrete, with adequate width to ensure slow flow rate, it should be possible to leave it so that it becomes the main stream channel permanently. The new dam then holds back an off-stream, rather than an on-stream pond, with all the advantages that this gives.

The inflow to such a pond can then be controlled, using pipes or sluices as described earlier in the section on off-stream ponds. There will then be much less need for flood overspill systems from the pond (provided it is certain that the stream will never overtop its new channel) and silting in the pond will be almost eliminated.

Water level control, flood overspill and pond drainage systems

A stream fed pool behind a dam will require some form of water level regulating structure for the outlet of excess water at normal flow, as well as a means of effecting complete drainage. Some pools will also need to have a facility for discharge of greater volumes of water during flood times; the need for this depends on the catchment area and local rainfall levels, and this must be considered in the design of the dam.

Spillways

For a pond made by damming a low volume stream serving a small catchment, where the range of flows in the stream is limited, a simple spillway can suffice for both normal overflow and flood flows, as in Figure 36. As such a spillway would be permanently flowing it must be surfaced, either with rock or slab paving or concrete on a firm rubble sub-base.

Where the range of flows is greater, the spillway can be made more complex to meet the dual purpose of normal outlet and flood

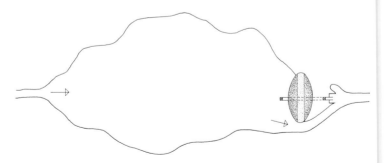

Figure 36. This pond, with a small catchment area, has a simple stone or concrete line spillway channel to take normal overflow and the small flood volumes.

overspill, ie a small channel is made and lined with stone or paved to take normal overflow, and this is set 20cm deep into a much wider, turf covered flood overspill channel (Figure 37).

An earth dam should have a minimum of 1m freeboard above normal water level, giving sufficient clearance so that in a storm waves will not overtop the dam, causing erosion. The sill level of any spillway should therefore be at least 0.6m below the dam crest and 0.3m above the level of the normal outlet.

It must, of course, be designed to cope with the maximum possible storm run-off from the entire stream catchment above the dam, otherwise floodwater will overtop the dam, erode the downstream face and cause the dam to fail. For dams in large catchments it is therefore wise to seek professional advice. Granfield 1971 (Forestry

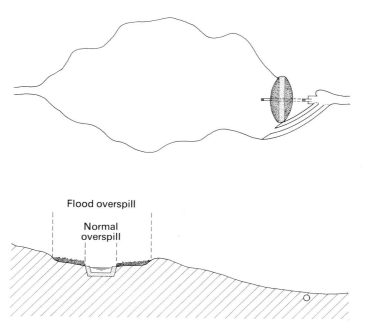

Figure 37. This pond, fed by a large catchment, has a dual height spillway. The deeper channel is stone or concrete lined to take normal overflow, and it is set into a wider turf lined channel which takes the larger flood flows.

Commission, Forest Record No.15) gives details of calculation of run-off from different catchments and in any event remember that a dam on a catchment area greater than 200ha will require a very complex flood spillway to be built and is not really worth considering for a farm pond or lake.

If the dam is made on a stream which trout, sea trout, salmon or coarse fish species run up to spawn, then it is important to provide them with a permanently flowing spillway designed so that they can negotiate it with ease. This can mean rather complex structures and readers should consult their Regional NRA Fisheries Officer (see Appendix 2).

It is important that a spillway should be made wide enough, with a suggested minimum width of 3m. This is because the flow rate will be less if the overflowing water is shallow. For the same reason, the inlet area should have a wide flare, to minimise flow rate over the sill, which can be a point subject to erosion.

Similarly, the gradient of the spillway channel should be as gentle as possible, preferably 1 in 40 or less, and it is particularly important to ensure an erosion-free point of return of flood overspill to the stream, so a stone or concrete apron should be built to act as a spreader where the overspill discharges to the stream below the dam. This can be equipped with vertical slabs, boulders, concrete posts or stakes to act as spreaders to scatter the water stream, reducing erosion potential. As with any outlet point, it should be built well away from the toe of the dam.

With relatively small floods from a catchment area of less than 15ha and where the soils are stable (ie good for dam building) there is no need to surface the spillway, it is sufficient to allow it to grow a good turf covering, preferably seeding it at an early stage. If the catchment is large, or if there is a possibility of large volumes of flood water at high flow rates, it is essential to line the spillway bed and sides with paving, stones or concrete to reduce the risk of erosion.

The spillway should be built during dam construction so that it takes water around the end and not over the surface of the earth dam.

Water level control through the under-dam pipe

If a permanent spillway overflow is not necessary, the pipe laid to contain the stream during dam construction can become, as is usual for small dam impoundments, the outlet for complete draw down of the pond if necessary, and at the same time it can serve as the outlet for normal overspill water via a controllable sluice or valve. In this case, the level control structure should be built at the upstream end of the pipe, in the deepest part of the pool, with the inlet turned up a little way to keep it clear of the bottom and with an erosion-preventing concrete or boulder and rubble apron made at the downstream outfall of the pipe – all made *before* the stream is diverted into the pipe. The lower outfall of the pipe should be led well downstream of the toe of the proposed dam.

The drainage pipe can be closed by a simple flap valve on the upstream end. This will be held closed by water pressure under normal circumstances and can be opened when required by a rope (permanently attached to the flap) from the surface. If a large buoy is attached to the bottom edge of the valve flap by a rope which only just reaches the surface, any rise in water level will then lift the buoy, open the valve and allow the surplus water to flow away – such a system could be used to make a small pond self-regulating, with an outflow only when necessary. Alternatively, the outlet could be regulated by means of a gate valve on the downstream end of the pipe. Figure 38 shows these alternatives.

Probably the simplest level control and drainage mechanism for small impoundments is to fit a right angle elbow joint to the upstream end of the pipe, with "O" ring seals, adding another length of pipe to this so that it is vertical (Figure 39).

The height of the open end of this pipe will determine the water level. To lower the level, the pipe simply has to be rotated on the elbow joint so that the upper end goes below the water surface, allowing an outflow until the level again reaches the level of the open end of the pipe. The upstream end of the pipe at the elbow joint should rest on a hard, clean surface, such as concrete paving slabs, and these should extend out to each side of the pipe end. This

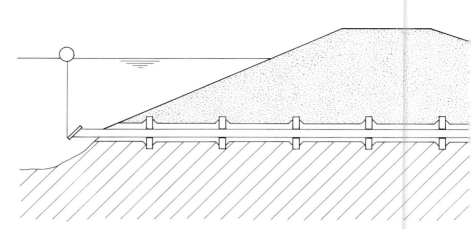

Figure 38. In small ponds, the outflow can be regulated by means of a flap on the upstream end, or a gate valve on the downstream end of the under-dam pipe.

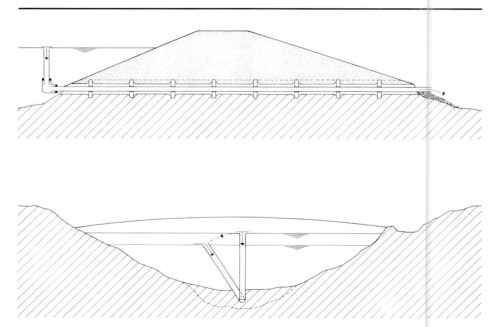

Figure 39. A rotatable vertical section of pipe on the upstream end of the under-dam pipe allows easy regulation of water level.

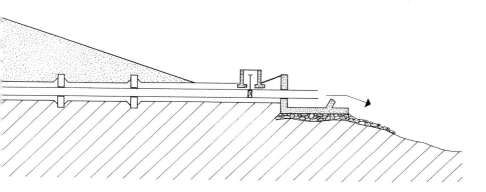

is so that the vertical pipe can be easily turned to lay horizontally and the hard paved area can be easily cleared of silt and detritus which might otherwise prevent full downward rotation of the pipe.

This upstand pipe should be at the upstream end of the pipe so that water pressure holds the joint together and pressure inside the pipe is low. It helps, therefore, to fit an eyebolt to the top of the pipe so that it can be moved by using a boat-hook from the shore. The inflow end of the pipe should be protected from blockage with flotsam by means of a mesh screen.

Being set in the deepest water, such a control system is less likely to be the target of vandalism, but if there is any danger of interference, the vertical pipe section can be chained and padlocked to a stout post set into the pond bed.

Water level control through a 'Monk' sluice

The very simple type of overflow outlet control described above is adequate where a 15cm pipe is capable of taking normal stream flows, bearing in mind that it should not be fully charged all the time.

If the pipe has to be larger than this, it becomes impractical to rotate it on the elbow joint and a more robust structure is required.

The usual solution, combining level control with full drainage facility in such cases, is to build a "monk" type sluice.

Monk sluices are ideal for ponds on streams with low to medium flow ranges, but can also be made with a pipe large enough to cope with fairly large flood flows. If the dam is on a spate stream, however, the monk can be combined with a flood spillway made with the sill 30cm above monk top board level and at least 60cm below the dam crest. (See section on spillway design.)

A monk sluice is basically an open-sided box, with a back wall and two side walls, each 15–22cm thick, made using shuttering and poured concrete, or built with bricks or solid building blocks on a substantial concrete base. The water in the pond produces an upthrust on such installations, proportional to the head of water. To counteract this, ensuring that the monk does not move or crack, the base should be as thick as half the head of water. For example, in a depth of 1.4m the concrete base should be 0.7m thick. It is usual to make the back wall 0.5m long, with each side wall being 1.0m. The top of the sluice should be about 30cm above normal water level, ie above the top of the uppermost sluice board but below the dam crest, the base sets the level of the outlet pipe and this should be at the lowest point to which it will ever be required to drain the pond. For a fish pond it is useful to build the monk in the base of a chamber in the pond bed, so this will act as a sump to collect fish as the water drains away. Figure 40 shows the details of construction.

The inner surface of each side wall has three vertical channels, either built in or of galvanised steel bolted to the walls and sealed on a mastic bed. These must lie exactly opposite each other, run from the top right down to the base, and the inner two must be able to take a sluice board (seasoned elm or oak) at least 25mm thick. These boards can be as deep as you wish; the water level is set by the height of the top board and the depth of each board governs the steps by which the water level can be altered. Shallow boards thus give a greater degree of level control. However, a larger number of shallow boards means more joints between them and this increases the loss of water by seepage.

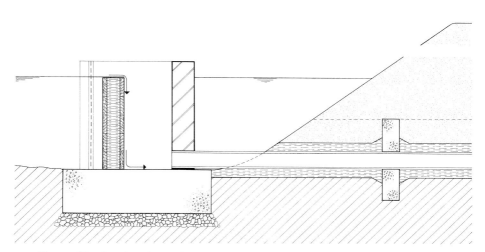

Figure 40a. Section through a monk sluice outlet.

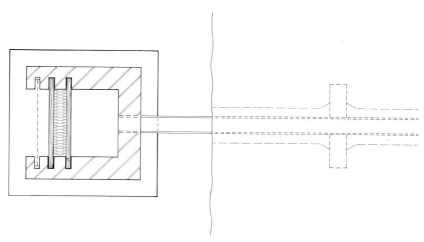

Figure 40b. Plan of a monk sluice outlet.

93

The reason for having two sets of channels and boards now becomes clear – the space between them can be packed with clay soil (or straw) to reduce seepage. The outermost channels take a metal grille, with vertical bars to prevent blockage of the monk outlet pipe by flotsam which might otherwise flow over the top board.

The base of the sluice should have the lowest board, which should only be a shallow one, sealed firmly to the concrete slab to form a low upstand, upon which the next board will rest. If this is omitted, it will be found that stones and other detritus accumulating on the floor of the monk can prevent the lowest sluice board from seating correctly if it is ever removed and then replaced.

Each board must have two eyebolts fixed to one of its faces so that it can be lifted out of its slot using a pair of long handled hooks. It is much easier to draw the boards up if there is one ring towards each end, rather than just one in the centre, as the board can be prevented from tilting in the channels, which can cause it to jam.

The water which flows over the sill of the top board falls in to a collecting chamber behind the inner set of boards and is carried under the dam by the pipe put in to take the original stream flow. This pipe should be a minimum diameter of 15cm and naturally it must be able to cope with normal flow when 20–30% full, and with the full flood flow when fully surcharged, unless it is combined with a secondary system in the form of a flood spillway. It is a good idea to cover the top of the monk with a lockable bar to prevent interference with the boards and hence unwanted drainage of the pond.

Water level control through an outlet chamber

As an alternative means of setting the water level and allowing excess water to leave the pond, one can install an outlet chamber near the shore, where the water is shallower and construction is simpler. Unlike the monk sluice the chamber type outlet provides a set water level only, with no facility to alter it at will.

Chamber outlets also differ from monk sluices (which have to

94

be built in the base of the pond) in that they can be made well up on the shore, providing the top of the chamber is 1m below the dam crest (and 30cm below the sill of the flood spillway if there is to be one). It can thus be built in dry conditions, before the water level is allowed to rise. Figure 41 shows the details of a simple outlet chamber.

The water collecting chamber itself can be made from concrete, bricks or concrete blocks, on a slab base which, like that for the monk sluice, should be as thick as half of the head of water at the chamber. It is also possible to build a chamber using concrete ring sections, as used to make manholes on sewerage and drain pipes. The chamber should be protected from flotsam by a surrounding mesh screen, easily supported on a timber framework.

The chamber outlet needs to have its own separate pipe laid from its base to carry away the overspill and it is best to lay this in the ground around the end of, rather than through, the dam itself. This outlet pipe from the chamber will need anti-seepage collars along its length, as for the under dam drainage pipe if there is one, and it should discharge its flow well downstream of the toe of the dam, on to a concrete or stone apron to prevent erosion.

The pipe should also be of a size able to carry away normal over-flow, and it is quite feasible with this system to make it large enough, say 30cm up to 2.0m diameter (spun concrete pipes), to take large volumes of flood water. If it is not practical to build it large enough to carry all of the floodwater, the primary chamber outlet should be combined with a secondary flood spillway, which should be at the opposite end of the dam. Figure 42 shows the correct location of monk sluices and outlet chambers.

Design and construction of earth dams

Having decided on the appropriate means of diverting the stream flow, and which type of water level and flood overspill system is needed for your particular situation, catchment area and stream flow characteristics, the next step in designing the dam is to deter-

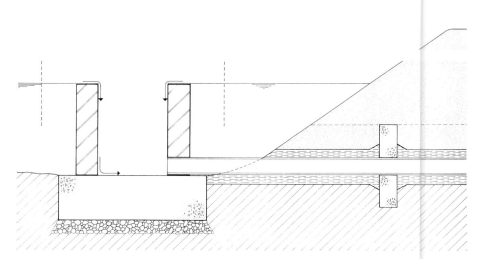

Figure 41a. Section through a pond outlet chamber.

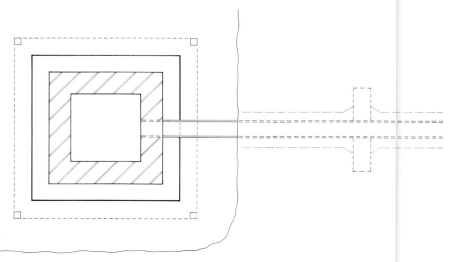

Figure 41b. Plan of a pond outlet chamber.

96

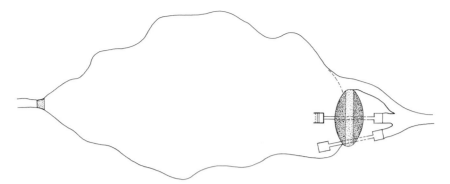

Figure 42. The monk should be built close to the dam in the deepest section of the pond. The outlet chamber can be alongside the shore, but should be at the opposite end of the dam to the spillway if there is one.

mine the height of the top level outlet or overflow, as this will set the water level and thus determine the area, shape and volume of the pool. The top or crest of the earth dam must then be built at least 1.0m above the normal water level.

Calculation of dam height and pool volume

To find the required height, place a "T" piece on the site of the dam, on the mid-point of the centre line, with the top of the T at the estimated height. You can then place more T pieces a little way upstream of this one, with their tops exactly level at the same height as the first. If you then sight across from the main T to each upstream T your sight line will intercept the land at the future water line, and you can have a helper to peg each point on the shore (Figure 43).

Alternatively you could use just one T piece at the dam and sight from the top of this using a telescopic rifle sight, checking it for level with a spirit level. Either way, you can peg out the rough outline of the water with an overflow at the chosen height of the dam T piece.

Once this is done it is possible to get a reasonable estimation of

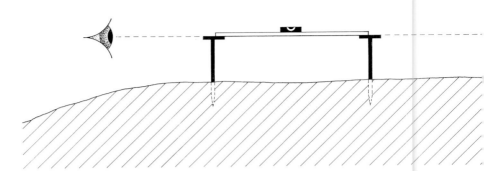

Figure 43. The height of dam needed to hold back a pond of the desired extent can be determined by sighting across two "T" pieces at the same level at the dam site. Remember to add 1.0 metre for freeboard.

the stored volume of water in the pond as outlined. For the normal pointed wedge shaped pond which results from damming a valley stream, one has to multiply the length of the pool (in metres) from the stream inlet to the dam face by the length of the dam at the waterline, then multiply the result by the water depth at the midpoint of the dam and divide the answer by six. (If the pond is rectangular or square, divide the answer by 3 and if it is more circular, divide by 2.5). This gives the volume of the pool in cubic metres and as one cubic metre equals approximately 225 gallons, it is easy to calculate the stored volume in gallons.

Remembering that it is best to avoid impounding a volume in excess of 5 million gallons, because of the complications in dam design, once the pool volume is known one can adjust the height of the dam accordingly. Although 5 million gallons of water does not seem very much, it will in fact cover a considerable area to a depth of 1-2 metres. For example, assuming the pool was uniformly 1.5m deep, with no marginal shallows, it could be almost 120m square (1.49ha) before exceeding the capacity of 5 million gallons, so it is unlikely that this volume would need to be exceeded where much of the pool is to be shallow.

Having selected the site, designed a dam of the appropriate height, with the necessary inlet, outlet, drainage and overspill structures,

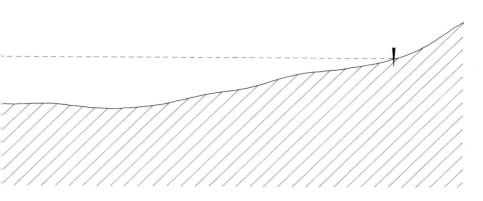

drawn up the plans and then gained licensing and approval for your proposals from the relevant authorities, you should (unless you plan to do the work yourself) seek tenders from a number of contractors who are experienced in this kind of work. Price and time estimates vary very widely for this sort of earthmoving, depending on the type of plant to be used, so it is wise to shop around. If possible you should examine other dams made by the tendering firms, and talk to their owners before choosing your contractor; the cheapest quote might not always be the best one to accept!

The contractor should first dig a number of trial holes at least 1.0m deep, or down into the top of the impermeable layer if it is less than this. These holes will reveal the nature of the underlying ground, exposing any weaknesses, such as previous gravelly stream beds or old land drains, and will indicate the type of dam that will be needed.

Site preparation

The entire area to be covered by the dam, including the valley sides where the ends of the dam will join them, *must* be stripped of all overlying vegetation, topsoil, porous sands or peat down to the sub-soil before dam building can begin. The stripped topsoil should be stored close to the dam so that it is convenient for use in finishing off the dam surfaces later.

If the trial holes revealed any lines of weakness such as porous seams, drains or old stream beds in an otherwise impermeable sub-soil, these should be dug out and backfilled with suitable compacted soil before starting to raise the dam proper.

General dimensions and proportions of earth dams

As mentioned earlier in the section on water level control structures and spillways, the crest of the dam should have at least 1.0m of freeboard above normal water level (unless the pond is very small). It must at least be sufficient to prevent overtopping of the dam at any time, otherwise erosion of the downstream face may severely weaken the structure. The height will have been selected to give the desired water area and it should be remembered that a height of 4.5m is the maximum permissible without the dam being designed by a Chartered Engineer.

To achieve the final height, the dam has to be built at least 10-15% too high to allow for the inevitable settlement. It will therefore need to be made slightly "hog-backed" – higher where it is deepest, in the centre of the dam.

As a rough guide, the base of the dam should be equal to approximately five times the dam height. Table 3 gives the recommended widths of the base and crest of dams for a range of heights, where the upstream side has a gradient of 1 in 3, and the downstream slope is 1 in 2, which are the recommended maximum slopes for earth dams.

Table 3 Recommended dam dimensions

"h" Max. height of dam crest	"t" Min. width of dam crest	Min. width of dam base
1.8m	2.4m	11.4m
2.7m	2.7m	16.2m
3.6m	3.0m	21.0m
4.5m	3.3m	25.8m

This relationship between height and width at the base means that most earth dams on valley sites have an elliptical shape, they are higher, and therefore wider in the centre, narrowing towards the ends as the width needed decreases with the decrease in height above original ground level.

If the dam is holding back only a small pool volume and low head of water, it can be built straight across the valley, as in Figure 44.

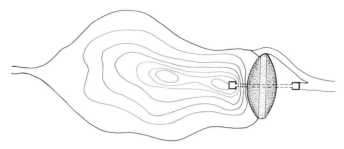

Figure 44. In a shallow, small volume pond, a low dam can be built straight across the stream course.

If the dam is a long, high one, holding back a lake with a large water volume, it should be made in an even radius curve which has its convex face on the upstream side. This creates an arch form, which is inherently much stronger than a curved dam which faces the other way, and this is seen all too often, ie with the concave face upstream. In the "arch type" dam, water pressure on the upstream face acts to compress the dam, forcing the ends into tighter contact with the valley walls (Figure 45).

Dam design in relation to building material quality and site characteristics

If the soil available for building the dam is homogeneous and of a suitable non-porous nature when compacted, the dam construction will be relatively simple. A straightforward earth embankment can be made and no impervious core structure will be needed.

101

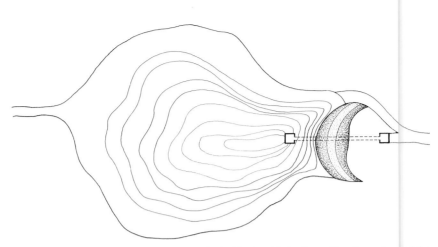

Figure 45. For a large volume pond, behind a high dam, the dam should be crescent shaped, with the convex face upstream.

If the subsoil on the dam is similarly non-porous, then there should be no problems. Once the site has been cleared, the subsoil surface which will be under the dam must be ploughed or disced to allow the dam base to key properly to it (Figure 46).

If the dam material is good, but the site is underlain by a permeable subsoil, the centre portion of the dam has to be extended downwards in a cut-off trench dug into the soil as far as the underlying impervious layer, usually clay or bedrock. As shown in Figure 47, this trench should be the first operation, dug at least 2.0m wide at its base, widening to two times the final dam height at the subsoil surface level. This trench is filled to ground level with compacted layers of the dam building material, preventing seepage loss under the dam.

It is also possible to prevent seepage loss through permeable under-dam soil layers by excavating a trench down to the impervious layer and filling it with concrete to make a cut-off wall. This should project up for at least 30cm from the subsoil surface so that it is keyed into the base of the dam as it is built over it (Figure 48). In large or high dams, however, this will need steel reinforce-

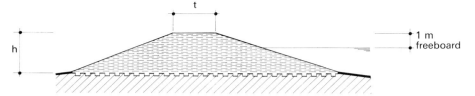

Figure 46. An earth dam built with good material on an impermeable subsoil is simply keyed in to the underlying layer.

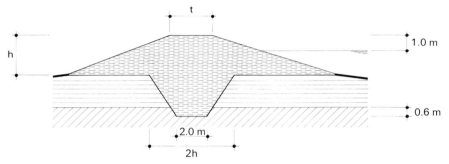

Figure 47. Where the subsoil is permeable, the centre of the dam must be extended down into the underlying impervious layer.

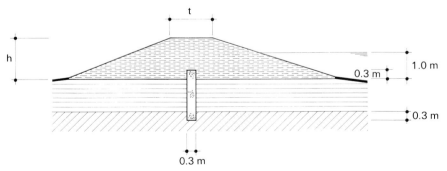

Figure 48. In some circumstances it may be simpler to build a concrete cut-off wall through the permeable layer.

103

ment and a Chartered Engineer should be consulted to ensure adequate design strengths are met.

If the only material available for building the dam is not of a high enough clay content, then the centre of the dam at least must be made with a high clay content (30–50% impervious material) to form a watertight core which is supported by the poorer material on each side. It is vital that the core is extended right out to the valley sides into which it should be extended, to key-in the ends of the dam.

If the core dam is built on an impervious layer, the core section should be keyed into it by cutting a trench along the centre line of the dam, across its full length, to a depth of 60cm. The width of the core in this case depends on the quality of the core material. If it is more than 50% clay its width at the base should be equal to the dam height, narrowing to half of the width of the dam top when it reaches the crest (Figure 49).

If the core material is 20–30% clay, the recommended minimum, the core at the dam base (subsoil surface level) should be twice as wide as the dam height, again narrowing to half of the top width at the crest (Figure 50).

The core section of the dam must be carefully filled and compacted, building up as the height of the dam is increased on each side.

If the core dam is built on a permeable layer, the clay core has to be extended downwards in a trench through the poor subsoil and at least 60cm into the impermeable layer, with a minimum width at the base of 2.0m and the same width at the soil surface and dam top as for the previous examples, depending upon the clay content of the core building material, as in Figures 51 and 52.

If your available core material is of a very high clay content, say 85–100%, then a vertical core wall of almost uniform width may be made of puddled clay as in Figure 53.

Such a core wall should be trenched at least 60cm into impermeable subsoil below the dam, through the permeable layer if there is one. The core is built in 15cm layers, each one carefully puddled and compacted as the dam height increases. In this case the very watertight nature of the core means that it can be the same width from the base to the dam top, but it is advisable to make it a minimum width of 60cm in the bottom of the trench, increasing to 1.0m wide at the subsoil surface on which the dam is to be built, from where it narrows as it rises to the dam top, where again it should have a minimum width of 60cm (Figure 54).

Method and conditions of working

The condition of the soil for building the dam is important. It should be in a damp, plastic state, neither too wet, as when you can squeeze water out of it, nor too dry, when it cannot be formed into a ball by squeezing it in the palm of your hand.

If the soil quality varies the best material, with the greatest clay content, should be used for the centre third of the dam. If there

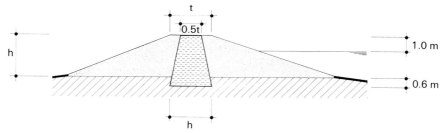

Figure 49. If the dam building material has a low clay content, it will need an impermeable core of higher clay content material.

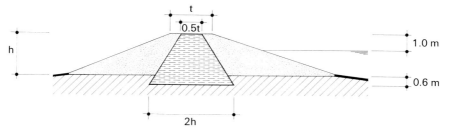

Figure 50. If the core material has a relatively low clay content it will need to be made wider.

105

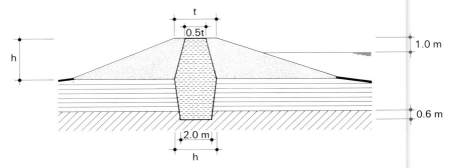

Figure 51. When a clay-cored dam is built on a permeable subsoil, the core must be extended down into the underlying impervious layer.

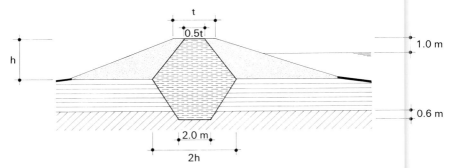

Figure 52. Here, too, if the core material has a relatively low clay content it will need to be made wider at the dam base.

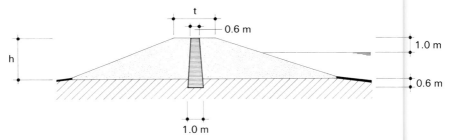

Figure 53. If the core material has a very high clay content the dam core can be made as a relatively narrow wall.

106

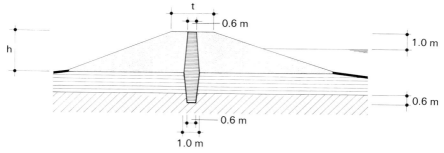

Figure 54. Where the dam is made on permeable subsoil, this core wall must be extended down into the underlying impervious layer.

are many rocks and stones in it they should be placed in the lower third during building, and they must be spread evenly and thoroughly compacted into the clay soil, not placed in piles which would later form points of weakness.

If at all possible the construction work should be done in summer, spreading the soil in layers no more than 15cm thick, and compacting each layer thoroughly before the next one is placed. A bulldozer blade is the best machine for this part of the work, but a tracked vehicle is not the best for compacting the soil, as ground pressure is usually quite low. A wheeled vehicle usually gives a much better result, and if the dam is of the type with a clay core, the core section at least should be compacted with a wheeled vehicle, mechanical tamper as used in roadworks, or a sheep's foot roller, the ideal tool for use on earth dams.

The dam should not be built in very wet weather as the water content of the soil can change later, causing shrinkage problems. Ideally, the surface of the work should be allowed to dry slightly before recommencing, and the surface should be disced or harrowed lightly between breaks to avoid separation of layers and the formation of seepage lines. If for any reason the work has to be halted, the dam should be left with a rounded, shouldered profile such that it sheds rainwater gently. Should the surface dry out between working periods, it must be watered lightly and again disced or harrowed before adding the next layer.

If you are obtaining material for the earth dam by excavation from the bed of the future pond, the excavation must be kept at least 3.0m away from the foot of the dam on the upstream side, and the face of the excavation near the dam should be at a maximum slope of 1 in 2 (Figure 55).

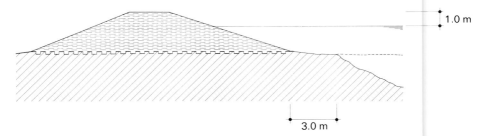

1.0 m

3.0 m

Figure 55. Any excavation upstream of an earth dam should be at least 3.0 metres from the foot of the dam.

Finishing off the earth dam

When the dam finally reaches its full height across the valley there is a great temptation to see the pond full. This must be resisted; the dam needs several months to settle and for the bare earth surfaces to develop a stabilising surface cover of vegetation.

This can be speeded up by covering the completed dam with the topsoil stripped from the site when work started. This can then be fertilized and seeded with a grass mixture. It is important to keep livestock off the dam until the turf cover is well developed and trees must not be planted anywhere on or near the dam as their roots can cause structural damage and seepage lines.

The dam face should be kept mown so that if there is any change in surface moisture level due to seepage it can be detected early, giving time to drain the dam and effect a repair at the earliest opportunity. Minor leaks in earth dams are a classic case where a "stitch in time" is needed – left alone they can only get worse, often surprisingly rapidly, hence the importance of including the under-dam draw down pipe!

108

If the dam is at the exposed end of a long stretch of water it will suffer from erosion by wave action. This should be guarded against by providing a log wave baffle as described in the section on plant establishment in Chapter 4, or by laying a stone paving or rip-rap facing on the dam face at the waterline, extending up far enough to allow for wave action at top flood water level.

Small stream weir dams

For less ambitions pond building projects, small streams may be dammed using a variety of materials, though it must be stressed that these are only to be used where the depth and volume of water to be impounded is very small.

Basically, what is needed in these situations is a weir which will slightly raise the water level in the upstream section. Suitable mixtures are: sandbags filled with a 4:1 sand and cement mix or clay soil; concrete blocks, slabs or brickwork on a suitable foundation; timber boards and stakes either alone, or as double rows packed between with earth; sleepers or telegraph poles; logs, bricks or rocks packed with earth, and timber supporting corrugated iron.

Provided they are built with a breakwater to resist erosion on the downstream side, where the water falls constantly, there are no very complicated requirements and their construction is largely a matter of common sense.

CHAPTER SEVEN

Restoration of Gravel Pits for Wildfowl

In Chapters 1 and 2 we pointed out the valuable role of gravel pits as new wildfowl habitats, and it is clear that they are becoming increasingly important in the field of creative conservation, where we are learning how to rebuild the habitats that have previously been destroyed. Gravel pits provide an excellent opportunity to redress the balance of wetland losses and thus to make a substantial contribution to the future welfare of wetland communities in Britain. The Game Conservancy Trust's research in this area is summarised in "Wildlife After Gravel", available from The Game Conservancy's Sales Centre at £19.45 (including p&p).

In creating these extensive new wetland areas we can manipulate the land and water so as to create many different types of aquatic habitat within the same water body. In this way we can produce a variety of conditions for the development of rich aquatic communities, from plankton to wildfowl, thus guaranteeing the future existence of lowland wetlands in Britain, together with the diverse populations of animals and plants which inhabit and depend on them.

Much of our farmland, especially in the Midlands and South-east, is gravel-bearing and as pressure on farmers to produce more food decreases it may become feasible to extract the aggregates to create new lakes. This can generate a considerable income, allowing the farm to acquire a lake at no cost apart, of course, from the loss of the agricultural production capacity of the worked land. Having a gravel pit lake also provides many opportunities for profitable after-use, be it for irrigation, fishing, shooting, general amenity and water sports, fish or crayfish production, while at the same time it is possible to integrate a degree of wildlife conservation value.

Ideally a large part, or indeed all, of the gravel pit would be restored and managed as wildfowl habitat. This is not always possible, but provided the lake is big enough, say 30ha and above, a substantial proportion may be set aside for conservation. This area should then become a separate zone, segregated from recreational activities. In this way the greatest effort and resources can be concentrated on one part of the site in order to achieve the ideal conditions and thus provide the maximum benefits to the wildlife community which will develop. The aim of the restoration work should be to create a lake basin which contains all of the features necessary to ensure that the area realises it full potential as wildlife habitat, so it should aim to provide the conditions described in Chapter 3.

Gravel workings which are to be restored as wildlife habitats must, of course, comply with legal obligations, not lead to any long-term financial drain, be aesthetically satisfying, be of true conservation value and should not conflict with other interests in the area. If carried out correctly this type of restoration will serve to enhance the operating company's reputation.

Planning legislation and gravel pits

The Town and Country Planning Act (1971) and the Town and Country Planning (Minerals) Act (1981) provide the legislative framework which controls the operation and restoration of gravel pits.

The nature of the restoration and type of after-use permitted for a particular gravel pit will relate in part to the policies defined in the relevant County Structure Plan and Local Plans. The Mineral Planning Authority has power to impose conditions on the method of working and restoration to be employed at a pit in order to ensure that operations are conducted in a fit and proper manner. When considering Planning Applications regarding gravel extraction the Planning Authorities are obliged to consult with statutory bodies such as the National Rivers Authority, English Nature, Scottish Natural Heritage, Countryside Council for Wales, Highways Departments, etc. who may recommend a restriction of activities or development of the site. It is therefore important to give consider-able attention to the details of site restoration and after-use at the time of the application for planning consent.

Planning the working and restoration

In order to achieve the best results from a scheme to create good wetland habitat from a gravel pit, a high degree of pre-operational planning is necessary. It will often be advantageous to integrate the restoration work with the working plan for the site. It is essential to determine what is practical with regard to the physical character-istics and operational requirements of the site.

The following issues will require early examination: the present flora and fauna; the nature, distribution and depth of the deposit; the intended method of extraction, phasing and time-scale of the operation; and the amount of overlying material (overburden) and topsoil. The volume of overburden, topsoil and any locally available inert fill, relative to the volume of the void created by removing the gravel, will determine the extent of the landform that it is pos-sible to create after excavation. It is, therefore, extremely important to establish this at an early stage.

Also important are the depth and variability of the water table, opportunities for water level control, and susceptibility of the site to seasonal flooding. These factors will have some influence on whether the site may be worked wet or dry. Where possible the area should be de-watered during the excavation and restoration phases. This will enable more efficient extraction of the mineral and reduces the amount of fine silt in the final lake, resulting in a better, more productive environment. Working the "pit" dry also allows finer control over the detail of the landforms that are made during restoration.

Where the details of the shape of the lake to be created are known and planned from the outset, it is possible to phase the working of the site to reduce earthmoving costs to a minimum. The aim should be to capitalise on the topographical features of the deposit wherever possible, using them to build in the desired physical features of the lake basin as described earlier in Chapter 3.

Use and disposal of silt

The disposal of the fine material contained in the gravel deposit is almost always a problem in gravel workings which are to be restored as wildlife habitat. It is very important to prevent it contaminating the basin of the final lake or adjacent rivers, as it has the long-term, adverse effect of making the water cloudy following windy weather, especially in shallow lakes. This, coupled with its soft, unconsolidated, unstable nature, means that the lake will be a poor site for submerged plant growth.

Where the mineral is extracted from a de-watered pit, the fine silt and clay fraction produced by the gravel washing plant can, however, be put to good use. If a clay retaining wall or bund is pushed up to isolate a section of the excavated area, the enclosed lagoon can be used to contain the silt, which settles out of suspension as the flow rate in the water stream from the washing plant falls. The cleaner water from this primary lagoon should be run off the top of the lagoon into an adjacent secondary settling lagoon, and if necessary into a third, before the clean water is allowed to run back into the lake in the first restored phase.

Once the silt level in the primary lagoon reaches the water surface, the outflow from the plant should be diverted to a new settlement lagoon, and the consolidated silt in the first site can be planted with *Phragmites* to develop into a valuable reed bed.

Progressive restoration procedure

A system of progressive restoration, where rehabilitation of each worked area proceeds while excavation of the next phase is in progress, speeds up the creation of the habitats, reduces the need for long term soil storage and reduces the time for which the site has to be de-watered, but it does depend upon careful planning.

Figures 56 and 57 show a gravel pit with each of the first four phases in a different stage of working or restoration.

Phase 1 has been completely worked out and restored using materials stripped off the top of gravel seam in phase 2, and is separated from phase 2 by a temporary bund so that it can be flooded without prejudicing the restoration of that phase. This means that the newly created habitat will be maturing while the remaining phases are being worked and restored. Each phase is separated by temporary clay bunds from the previously worked one in a similar manner as excavation proceeds across the site, and each phase is restored using overburden and topsoil removed from the next one, apart from the final phase, which uses up the material stripped off phase 1 at the start. This is the only material which needs to be stored. If the projected life of the pit is very long, necessitating an over-long storage period for the topsoil from phase 1, this can be used to restore an intermediate phase, the material for the top of the intermediate phase being stored to eventually restore the final phase.

Soil handling and site after-care

For any restoration to be really successful, the characteristics of the soils to be moved and their response to handling under different conditions must be understood. The damage caused to soil structure by earthmoving plant operating in wet conditions, or by unsuitable storage, is extremely difficult if not impossible to rectify, and if the soils available for restoration are degraded by maltreatment the quality of the restoration possible will be severely reduced.

Soils to be used to create new landforms should be stripped and placed immediately onto their final location, without compaction (as described in Chapter 6 in the section on disposal of spoil), or they should be stored in low heaps for the minimum possible time. If storage time has inevitably to be extended it is a good idea to seed the soil heaps with a grass mixture.

The Town and Country Planning (Minerals) Act 1981, also allows

114

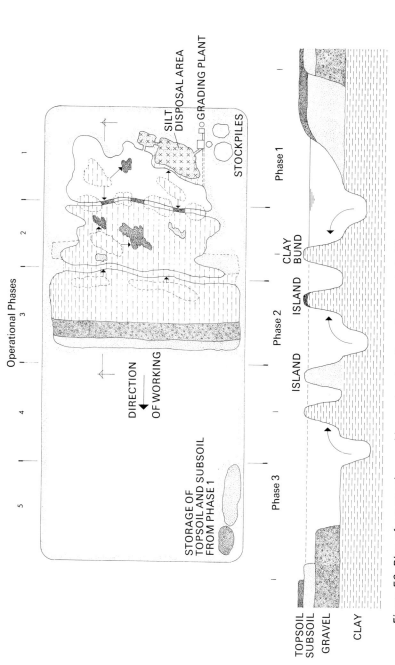

Operational Phases

STORAGE OF
TOPSOIL AND SUBSOIL
FROM PHASE 1

DIRECTION
OF WORKING

SILT
DISPOSAL AREA

GRADING PLANT

STOCKPILES

Phase 3   Phase 2   Phase 1

TOPSOIL
SUBSOIL
GRAVEL

CLAY

ISLAND   ISLAND

CLAY
BUND

Figure 56. Plan of progressive working and restoration of a gravel pit. Phase 1 is restored using overburden from Phase 2, and is already flooded. Phase 2 is being restored while still pumped dry, using overburden stripped from Phase 3. The clay bund between Phase 1 and Phase 2 will eventually cut into a chain of islands, allowing water to fill Phase 2 when its restoration is complete. Phase 3 is protected by a clay bund so that it can be worked and restored while water is kept pumped out.

Figure 57. Section through the above progressive working and restoration. Phase 3 is being reworked, Phase 2 is being restored and Phase 1 has been restored and flooded.

115

the Mineral Planning Authority to impose conditions on the after-care of the excavated site for a period of five years. Subsequent developments of the after-use of restored sites are usually dealt with by the District Councils. The after-care conditions will be related to such things as cultivating, seeding, fertilising, tree, shrub and aquatic planting, weed control, mowing, land drainage and fertilising. The main aim of the after-care conditions will be to ensure that the site receives a standard of care adequate to ensure that soil structure, fertility, drainage etc. develop properly and that the site becomes fit for the designated after-use.

The scope for habitat creation in gravel pits extends beyond just the lake itself. They also provide the opportunity for the recreation of a range of habitats and native species reintroductions. Because of the scale of earthmoving and reshaping of the land surface involved in gravel extraction, it is possible during the production and restoration operations to arrange suitable sites for the creation of new woodland, scrub, carr, wet grassland flower-rich meadows and in some cases heathland. Indeed, the scale of loss of lowland riverbank wet grassland is such that it is a habitat which should now be recreated wherever possible. It may prove difficult to recreate such habitats as exact replicas, species for species with their natural counterparts, but it is possible to get very close.

In conclusion, lowland gravel pits provide many opportunities for the recreation of useful habitats for wildlife. Provided the details are worked out carefully at the very early stages, and that the excavation and restoration works are carried out with due regard to the conditions of the site, eg the soil types, water table and nature of the deposit, and to the precise features needed in the chosen habitat, these new habitats can be remarkably valuable and productive.

CHAPTER EIGHT

Management of Ponds and Lakes to Maintain and Improve Habitat for Wildfowl

What is management?

Management of a body of water is the control of conditions to ensure that they meet the needs of the "target" plant and animal communities. This means either instituting changes to provide the necessary conditions or preventing predictable changes from occurring in order to keep the conditions, ie maintenance of required habitats.

The aims of management

The objectives of management should be to provide for all of the nature conservation values present on the site, increasing species diversity and maximising its contribution to the wildlife of the area. Thus, once it has been established that management is necessary to maintain a wetland, it can be seen that the management process may be aimed achieving a wide variety of results.

Management may be to restrict the effects of people using the site; to ensure survival of a particular rare species; to create sanctuaries or refuges; to increase waterfowl production, or to enhance the value of the site as a scientific, aesthetic or sporting resource. The aims depend ultimately upon the wishes of the owner and manager.

Why is management necessary?

Management is necessary because conditions within and around a pond are not stable. Nature alters the situation as different plant communities develop with time, in a process known as succession. Each plant community changes the conditions around it to favour another, usually more robust one, in a recognised and therefore predictable series. Thus, open water becomes weed choked and shallower so that reed swamp and then fen vegetation invades; willows and alders seed themselves into this as the soil level rises and within a few years your lovely shallow pond is a wet scrubby woodland or carr. Ultimately on fertile soils this will develop into a dry woodland, or in poor acid soils in areas of very high rainfall, a raised bog. The various stages in the succession of habitats across a wetland are shown in Figure 58.

The need for a pre-management survey

Before any management work is begun, it is essential to carry out a survey of the water body. This should establish the existing conditions and provide information upon which management decisions may be based.

Factors that should be examined are: the nature of the catchment and the water supply – is it reliable? The water quality – are there any sources of pollution, is it nutrient-poor and acidic, or nutrient-rich and alkaline? Is the range of depths satisfactory? If there is a dam, is it sound? Are the shorelines stable, or eroding? Does the water receive adequate sunlight? Are there too many overhanging trees casting shade and adding excess leaf litter? What is the ratio of open water to aquatic plant stands? Which species of plants are present and how are they distributed? What animal species are present, and how do they use the site? What is the conservation value of the site at a local, county or even national level? What features make it of value to the landscape, how does it fit in with the surrounding countryside? There are so many areas to include in pre-management surveys that it is probably best to call in expert help to ensure that all the necessary relevant information is collected accurately. It would be a great pity to institute management which destroyed a really valuable habitat or endangered a rare species through failure to appreciate that it was there.

118

(Photo: Laurie Campbell/NHPA)

Britain needs sufficient wetlands to accommodate the many waterfowl which arrive each winter.

Good quality ponds should offer a useful wildfowl breeding habitat.

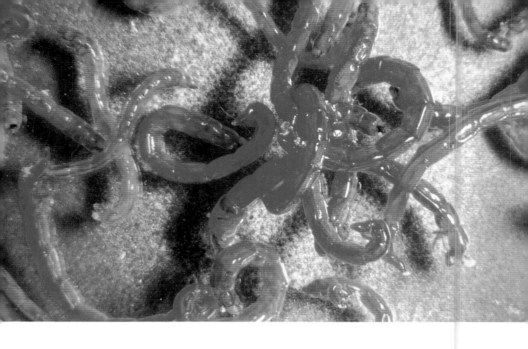

Invertebrates provide a vital food source for wildfowl, and especially growing ducklings.

Fish such as bream are significant predators of invertebrates which might other-wise feed ducklings.

Ducks will travel very long distances in search of insect-rich brood rearing habitats.

A well-managed wetland should offer a wide diversity of habitats.

Natural nesting cover such as offered by long grasses is essential to keep predation losses to a minimum.

Where natural cover is scarce, artificial nesting boxes and baskets can help.

Wildfowl value safe resting places where they can see approaching danger.

Good wetland management will help to conserve many other species such as snipe and frogs.

Planting up of new wetlands helps to establish diversity while at the same time restricting colonisation by invasive species.

Productive wetlands often become overgrown very quickly. Active management is essential to maintain diversity.

Regular daily feeding and not overshooting are the keys to attracting good numbers of birds to a small flighting pond.

The fruits of good management. There is no reason not to take a modest harvest from a well-maintained wetland.

Is management of your site necessary?

Having made the detailed survey, you have to decide whether any management is necessary at that time or in the future. This will, of course, depend upon the objectives of that management and the intended use of the water body.

The survey should enable you to answer such questions as which plants, if any, need to be controlled? Should additional species be established; if so, which ones? Do the shorelines or pond bed need alteration; is there too much disturbance and does the pond need more shelter? One must also consider whether the conditions on the banks and in the area surrounding the water meet the desired objectives. In this way it is possible to assign priorities to the various tasks which may be deemed necessary.

If management action is considered to be required then it should be carefully planned in order to arrange the various tasks at the appropriate season. It should be possible to minimise the short term damage caused to pond communities by, for example, plant removal, by limiting the work to small blocks, completing the job over a number of seasons. In this way, unaltered plant and animal communities remain to recolonise the managed sites as they settle down.

Opportunities for management

Management work has to be concentrated on the areas where it will be most effective. Some of the features of existing wetland habitats are difficult or impossible to manipulate, for example the geographical location, but in making new waters the actual site can be selected with due regard to the eventual management aims, and the size, shape and soils of the basin can be modified to ensure that the water body has the potential to develop along the desired lines.

The impact of human activities is obviously subject to management and the nature of such damage limitation is largely common sense. The plants on the banks and water margins will quickly be

Figure 58. The plant zones across a pond shore gradually invade the open water in a process of habitat change called succession.

120

Direction of Succession of habitats

destroyed by any repeated trampling, so any recreational activities can conflict with conservation where the water is used intensively. Once the vegetation cover is destroyed at points of access to the water the banks will rapidly erode. This can be particularly true where anglers cut seats out of the bank and in such cases it is essential to limit public access to specific sections of the shore, with either permanent closed sections or by allowing access to different sections each year.

For the most part, wetland management involves control of various components of the biological system. Thus one may influence the water supply, water quality, plant nutrients, soils and, to a certain extent, the amount of sunlight reaching the pond. The main part of the system where control is normally most effective, however, is the plant community in and around the water. Control of the vegetation is without doubt the major tool at the disposal of the wetland manager. Plant community or system orientated management, based on natural successional patterns, produces the most ecologically and economically sound results. The manager does need an understanding of how the various species of wildfowl and other wildlife use the area, how these are affected by the dynamic processes operating in a wetland and how these processes may be manipulated for the benefit of wildlife. Chapter 3 provides guidance on the conditions that need to be established and maintained in order to maximise benefits to wildfowl.

Management of the vegetation

In the early years of wetland development, the emphasis will be on the establishment of rich and diverse vegetation in and around the pond as described in Chapter 4. However, with the passage of time, and in a small, shallow pond this can be as little as five or six years, this vegetation will become too much. As a result of the process of succession described earlier, the water area will begin to become too restricted and overgrown for waterfowl to use. As a general rule they prefer wetlands which are maintained in the earlier stages of succession, with at least 60% open water to 40% vegetated area, and stopping succession at an early stage also gives longer lasting benefits, while maintaining a high diversity of ecological niches.

Management of a pond or lake will therefore change with time, from initial encouragement of the aquatic vegetation to control and removal of it! The main problem almost always is the invasion of shallow water feeding areas by marginal plants such as reedmace, common reed and reed sweet-grass (*Glyceria maxima*). All three are best avoided altogether on small ponds as they are so invasive.

Criteria for the selection of management method

It should be clear by now that the usual role of the wetland manager is to accelerate, maintain or retard the rate of succession of the vegetation communities in and around the water in order to create and keep the desired conditions that will support a wide range of species at relatively high densities.

The method of management of the vegetation selected to do this should be based on the following guidelines: will it be possible with the available finance, time and labour? Will it meet legal requirements and need approval from the relevant authorities? Is it likely to result in excessive disturbance to wildlife and most important, will it achieve the desired objectives?

Reduction of nutrient supply

Excessive growth of water plants is almost always the result of high nutrient levels, where the amount of nitrates and phosphates in particular are elevated above normal. The first step in controlling weed growth should therefore be to eliminate, or reduce as far as possible, all sources of nutrients entering the water. Field drains, streams and ditches will carry in fertilisers leached from their catchments and dairy, piggery and silage effluents are very detrimental in this respect. They must be kept out of water-courses. Excessive leaf litter from surrounding trees will also add considerable amounts of plant nutrients to a pond.

Whenever the growth of water plants is controlled, it very often appears that one weed problem becomes replaced by another! This is because of their ultimate dependence on nutrient supply for growth, given that they receive adequate light. Thus, if the rooted pondweeds are prevented from growing, the nutrients that they would have absorbed from the water will still be present, and will be diverted into some other form of plant growth, usually single-celled planktonic algae or blanketweed.

It is probably best, therefore, to aim at limiting nutrient supply, as above, and to remove excess plant material (either freshly cut or when dead) from the water, thus stripping nutrients from the water. The removed material should be burned or composted well away from the water, or the nutrients released will find their way back into the pond.

Some work by The Game Conservancy Trust at the ARC Wild-fowl Centre in the mid 1970s involved the addition of barley and wheat straw to newly flooded gravel pits as a means of increasing the populations of invertebrates which are important as wildfowl foods. It was observed during early trials of this technique that straw treated sites remained crystal clear, while adjacent untreated pools developed the usual algal blooms. It was therefore assumed that the bacterial decomposition of the straw absorbed (as it does in terrestrial conditions) considerable amounts of nitrates and phosphates from the surrounding water, thus denying them to the algae and limiting their growth. Similar observations were made at the same time by a farmer whose hay bale duck hide had fallen into the inlet stream of his pond. As is the way of such things, the bales were left "until some other time" before they were removed, and thus they remained. The following season the farmer noticed that his pond did not suffer from its normal spring overgrowth of blanket weed.

These two observations were followed up by the Aquatic Weeds Unit of the Weed Research Organisation, who subsequently demonstrated significant reduction of plant nutrients, in particular of phosphate phosphorus, in water which had flowed through a straw mass. The effect was most marked once the straw had been colonised by invertebrates such as freshwater shrimps and snails, which grazed the bacterial film increasing its rate of growth and cell division. The straw also appears to contain an algistatic compound which serves to limit algal growth.

It is possible to use this phenomenon to reduce plankton blooms in certain situations. The inflow stream to a pond can be made to flow through a "baffle" of straw bales placed along the stream bed. The bales will absorb quite a lot of the dissolved nutrients, reducing algal growth and produce quantities of duck and fish food organisms. It is essential, however, to remove the bales at the end of the summer, otherwise they will break up, wash into the pond and add their nutrient load to the water.

Physical removal

All water plants may be controlled to some extent by mechanical means, and physical removal by digging them out is both selective and effective if done thoroughly, but it is slow and labour intensive. It is also difficult to do in deep water and causes much disturbance within the water body, stirring up sediments, releasing plant nutrients and possibly causing de-oxygenation, particularly if it is done when the water is warm.

Repeated cutting and hoeing can be done in deeper water. Cutting also in many cases simply results in faster regrowth of the plants. If this method is used, it is essential to remove the cut material from the water, and it must not be left to rot on the banks. In the water it will decay and cause de-oxygenation and nutrient enrichment; left on the banks, the run-off water will carry nutrients back into the pond with the same results. Remember, any excess nutrients in the pond will cause planktonic algal blooms and further de-oxygenation and stagnation.

Chemical control

To advocate the use of herbicides in and around water bodies causes many conservationists to protest in horror! However, most of their fears are misplaced, herbicides which are approved for use in or near watercourses are proven to be non-toxic to fish and invertebrates and are not of long-term persistence in the environment. They are, in the main, very effective, simple to use and safe for the operator and the environment, **provided the manufacturers' instructions are properly complied with.**

A major advantage of herbicides is that they require much less time and labour to achieve more complete control than physical removal, meaning that the necessary management work is much more likely to be done, with all of its benefits to the habitat and wildlife. Also, they involve much less widespread disturbance to the habitat and bird life than physical disruption of plant beds, and the end result is much the same; if a bed of water plants is removed physically or chemically, it is still gone. With herbicide use, the invertebrates associated with the plants also have a chance to migrate to new niches as their host plants die, whereas with physical removal many of the insects disappear with the plants.

A disadvantage is that they are not as selective as the physical methods and their use in wildlife management does require a great deal of caution. For example, steps can be taken to save desired species by transplanting specimens out of the area to be sprayed, and by only treating a small block each season. They must also be applied at the correct stage of growth and in the correct dilutions as given by the manufacturer. For most aquatic plants, the most effective time to spray is when they are reaching their midsummer growth peak, just before flowering. This however can easily result in a sudden die-off of large amounts of plant tissue in warm water, causing de-oxygenation problems. In conservation areas and fisheries therefore, it is best to apply herbicides early in the season, when the plants are actively growing but before weed beds become very dense. In practice most herbicides can be applied effectively any time between June and mid-September.

A knapsack sprayer, or in smaller areas with difficult access, a hand held pump-up garden sprayer, is the ideal means of liquid application. Where control needs to be more selective it is possible to use a weed-wiper or herbicide glove applicator. The granular herbicide Dicholobenil (trade name Casoron G & G-SR) is good for spot treatments, as it acts via the lake soil upon which it is spread so its effect is localised.

If you do consider the use of herbicides in or around ponds, you must only use those which are approved for use in or near watercourses. The most suitable aquatic herbicides are "Roundup" from Monsanto Ltd and "Spasor" from May & Baker, both of which are glyphosate; "Clarosan" from Ciba Geigy, the active ingredient of which is terbutryne; "Prefix", which is chlorthiamid; "Dow Dalapon" by Dow Chemicals Ltd; "Reglone" or "Midstream" both formulations of diquat from ICI Agrochemicals; and "Casoron G & G-SR", which is dichlobenil, also made by ICI Agrochemicals Ltd.

Before any spraying you must first identify the weed and determine that it is not a rare or endangered species, then choose an appropriate herbicide and prepare and apply it in strict accordance with the manufacturer's instructions.

Those species of plant which have aerial leaves are most easily controlled by a glyphosate spray (Roundup or Spasor). Dalapon will also kill grass type emergent reeds. There are two notable exceptions which are not easily controlled by glyphosate, these are marestail *(Hippuris vulgaris)* and arrowhead (*Sagittaria sagittifolia*), both of which should be treated with dichlobenil.

Floating-leaved plants (except broad-leaved pondweed, *Potamogeton natans*) are susceptible to glyphosate, dichlobenil, chlorthiamid, diquat and terbutryne. These latter three also control submerged plants, and the last two also control free floating plants such as duckweed and blanket week algae. Broad-leaved pondweed is fairly susceptible to diquat and terbutryne but may need repeat treatments for full control.

Blanket weed (filamentous green algae) and duckweed may be a problem in an organically rich pond, particularly if it interferes with fishing or becomes so dense that it cuts off the light to the submerged plants. The ducks do not mind it – in fact they will eat the duckweed – but if duckweed is present in excess it may be removed physically (it makes excellent compost), or it can be readily controlled with glyphosate, diquat or terbutryne.

Blanket week (algae) may be raked out of the pond, or killed off using terbutryne granules (Clarosan). If it is raked out it must not be left to rot on the pond margins, the run-off as it decays is almost as polluting as silage effluent! The use of terbutryne will also kill most other submerged plants, which may not be altogether desirable, except perhaps in the case of clearing fishing swims. This granular weedkiller is thus best used as a spot treatment, clearing a small area each year. If the spot treatments result in a massive die-back of plants, their subsequent decay in the water can cause severe de-oxygenation problems for the animal life in the pond, so it must be used with care. Ideally weed overgrowth problems should be anticipated and treatment carried out early in the season to effect a kill before the plant mass becomes too large (this also means that treatment is more effective and less costly).

If the pond is an SSSI you must consult the relevant Government body before carrying out any vegetation control (or other management work). In an enclosed pond or lake it is not normally necessary to obtain NRA clearance to use approved herbicides, but local byelaws vary so it is worth checking. Permission *is* necessary if the pond has an outlet flowing to a water course of any kind.

The normal requirement in such cases is that the water level should be lowered before treatment with herbicide, such that there is no discharge to the water course for at least 10 days after spraying. If there is any doubt it is wise to seek expert advice and The Game Conservancy's Advisory Service can help here. The Ministry of Agriculture, Fisheries and Food also produces an excellent handbook called 'Guidelines for the use of herbicides on weeds in or near watercourses and lakes', which is available from MAFF Publications, Lion House, Alnwick, Northumberland NE66 2PF. Specialist advice on the use of herbicides to reduce water weed problems may also be obtained from the Aquatic Weeds Research Unit, c/o Department of Applied Zoology, University of Reading, Whiteknights, Reading, Berkshire.

The use of water depth

The growth of plants is ultimately controlled by sunlight level, and this factor can be used to effect a measure of control. If you can reduce the amount of light reaching part of the water area, then the aquatic weed growth in that spot will be much reduced. Light is rapidly absorbed by water and the effect of this can be seen in deeper pools, which in almost all circumstances, except where the water is exceptionally clear, will be weed-free if deeper than 5–7m, and very often only 2–3m of depth will eliminate most submerged species.

The new water area should therefore contain suitably situated deeper areas, for example as fishing swims, fish refuges and diving duck feeding sites. The spread of invasive aquatic plants like reed-mace (*Typha latifolia*) and reed sweet grass (*Glyceria maxima*) can also be checked if they are planted on shores which shelve off quickly into water more than 2m deep.

The effect of shading

In some cases one or two high light demanding, water loving trees, such as common alder or white willow, can be planted at the water-side on the south bank of the pond, so that the shade that they cast over the water will reduce or even eliminate weed growth in that section. This is only recommended for fairly large waters. In a small pond, say less than 0.5ha, the leaf litter from the trees could cause too much enrichment.

In shallow waters which become completely choked by sub-merged or floating-leaved plants, very effective and absolute local control can be achieved by the use of black plastic sheeting to prevent weed growth. This method is non-toxic, relatively cheap and easy to apply, and is extremely good for creating weed-free fishing swims, or patches of open water in dense weed beds, increases the productive "edge" and is much appreciated by fish, invertebrates and waterfowl.

A 500g or 1000g black polythene sheet, such as a rick sheet, preferably with eyeletted edges, has suitable weights (eg bricks) tied closely to each corner and, if it is large sheet, to points along the sides. This has then to be laid on the shore along the outer edge of the area to be treated, so that it eventually lays on the bank in a loose, elongated heap, parallel to the waterline (Figure 59).

The sheet has then to be pulled over the pond bed, using ropes attached to the waterside corners, pulling these out and away from the shore by using two boats so that it is stretched out fully over the selected area.

The sheet needs to be perforated at intervals, particularly near the centre, otherwise gases from the decomposing weed and the pond bed sediments will cause it to balloon up towards the surface. This problem can also be avoided if tightly woven black plastic

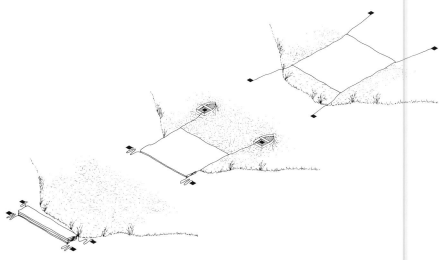

Figure 59. Laying a black lightproof sheet over a pond bed will eliminate any "weed" problems caused by excessive growth of water plants.

130

(polypropylene) mesh fabric is used instead of polythene sheet. This is equally effective.

It is essential to select the areas to be treated as soon as weed problems arise. In this way a control programme can be put into effect in the following season, before the weeds reach nuisance proportions. The shade sheeting will kill off the existing aquatic plants that it is put over, but it is far better and easier to put it in place early in the season, before the weeds begin to grow from their overwintering stages.

Once the area under the sheet is guaranteed weed-free and it is too late in the season for a dense growth to occur, ie by mid to late August, it is possible to move the sheet along to an adjacent patch to be in place ready for the following season. It usually takes a couple of years for each treated patch to revegetate significantly, so if necessary the sheet treatment can be used as a sort of rotation around the pond, clearing different spots each season. When the cost of various weed control methods is compared over a number of years, shading with black polythene sheet proves to be the least expensive.

Control by coarse fish

Limitation of submerged plant growth by reducing light levels can also be achieved through stocking heavily with bottom-feeding fish, although this is only really effective in ponds and lakes with relatively soft, silty sediments. The feeding activity of large populations (more than 250kg per ha) of bream, carp and, to a lesser degree, tench can stir up the sediments to such a degree that the water becomes permanently cloudy, thus significantly reducing light penetration and adversely affecting plant growth. The degree of this effect may be difficult to control, however, and the plant nutrients present in the fishes' waste products almost always result in increased blooms of planktonic algae, which further cloud the water and can eliminate rooted aquatic plants. The fish population will therefore need to be carefully managed in order to retain the required balance of weed growth and open water, and such control methods are not really compatible with trout fisheries, as the water becomes too turbid.

It is worth noting that there is considerable demand, and high prices are paid, for good quality fishing for specimen carp, tench and bream, and that large specimens of these species can be readily sold for restocking angling waters at very good prices, so it is possible to achieve a degree of weed control and make a profit from selling the fish once they have done the job!

Grass carp

In recent years there has been a great interest in the use of Grass Carp (*Ctenopharyngodon idella* Val.) for the biological control of aquatic weeds. Quite a lot of research has now been completed on the habits of this species and on its effectiveness as a weed control agent, and in some circumstances it can be very good. Although their effects may be uncertain, and their waste products may help to stimulate planktonic algal blooms, they do have some advantages.

They can survive in a very wide range of environmental conditions, will not breed in the wild in this country (certainly not in stillwaters at least), and so are not a threat to native species; they require little labour or attention once stocked, are low in cost compared to physical and chemical methods and they can be effective over a long period of time. They are also quick growing, with a maximum weight of around 12kg and the potential of very young fish to increase in weight six or seven-fold in only two (warm) seasons; they are a hard fighting, excellent sport fish, and are good to eat!

Unfortunately, they only feed really heavily once the water temperature rises to above 16°C, being most active for the short period in summer when waters can be expected to reach 20°C and above. Also, one can not dictate to a grass carp which pondweed to eat,

132

and their effects are therefore weather-dependent, unpredictable and non-selective.

In general they prefer to eat the softer plants, such as duckweed, Canadian pondweed, starwort, the finer leaved *Potamogeton* pondweeds, such as fennel-leaved pondweed (*P. pectinatus*) and stonewort. In the absence of these, eg when they have cleared them all, they will also eat milfoil, water crowfoots, hornwort, marestail, water mosses and blanket weed algae. If really short of food they have been known to eat some of the marginal reeds and in exceptional circumstances have been seen to feed on waterside grasses dangling into the water along the banks of fen dykes!

It is clear from this that in a small, shallow pond or lake, which is sheltered from the wind so that the water will warm up significantly in the summer, a population of grass carp can keep weed growth under control. The effectiveness of the fish and degree of control exerted obviously depends upon the amount and type of weed growth, stock density and the weight of fish per unit area of the pond.

The normal approach is to stock with an initial density of 200kg per hectare, using fish of around 100g to keep costs down, and relying on the fish to grow, effecting more weed control as their biomass increases.

As the size of the stocked fish increases with time, the stage will be reached where the weedbeds start to become overgrazed, at which time some of the carp need to be removed. The resale value of large specimens of grass carp is high, thus allowing the owner to recoup some of the initial outlay on stocking. They are notoriously difficult to net, being very good at leaping over nets, and if one goes, the rest often follow like a flock of sheep. Their management is much easier if the water is drainable – another good reason for including this facility.

Any water stocked with grass carp should not contain large numbers of pike, or the carp will quickly be eaten. If pike are present and cannot be removed, the stocked grass carp should be large, at least 2kg in weight.

As described in Chapter 10, the movement of fish in Britain is controlled by Section 30 of the Salmon and Freshwater Fisheries Act (1975) and any proposal to introduce grass carp must be approved by the Regional Water Authority's Fisheries Section. Being an exotic species, grass carp introductions are also covered by Section 14 of the Wildlife and Countryside Act (1981), and so approval and a licence to introduce them has to be sought from the Ministry of Agriculture, Fisheries and Food. Permissions are currently being granted for suitable sites, in particular for enclosed waters with no connection (temporary or permanent) to any flowing watercourse, and each case will be considered carefully.

The best way to find out about local suppliers of grass carp is to contact the Fisheries Officer of your regional National Rivers Authority office.

Management of reedbeds

If you are fortunate enough to have, or to be able to plant, a large area of common reed (*Phragmites australis*), this too will need careful management to retain its optimum value to wildfowl and other wetland wildlife. Many species of marshland bird require good reedbeds for successful breeding, and it is a most attractive habitat.

The best conditions for marsh birds are extensive reedswamp with scattered patches of open water, giving lots of reedbed edge, together with more open, wet, muddy areas with a more varied marsh plant community. Common reed is a vigorous plant and any area of water shallow enough for it to thrive, over a fertile soil, will rapidly become covered by it, reducing its value to wildlife. Left unchecked the reedswamp leaf litter will raise soil levels, dry out the marsh and progress through carr to woodland, so this excessive development of reeds needs to be prevented.

The simplest method of controlling reedswamp invasion of the open water and mud areas is to use the herbicide "Dalapon" or alternatively glyphosate at any time between May and August, but to reduce disturbance to nesting birds it is best to carry out the spraying after the middle of July. The herbicide should be applied to a one to two metre wide bank along the edge of the bed where it is encroaching on the open patches. Any regrowth in the following year may be easily controlled by spot treatments.

A reedbed can be maintained in good condition by regular cutting outside the growing season. A section of the bed should be cut annually so that each part is cut once every two to three years. This keeps the reeds growing vigorously, reduces the build up of leaf litter as the cut reeds are removed, increases plant species diversity and prevents the invasion of the reedswamp by woody scrub.

Provided it can be done in a controlled way, burning a reedbed in very early spring has the same effect. This is best done when there is quite a lot of moisture in the base of the reedbed to prevent too hot a burn at rhizome level.

Management of tree and shrub cover

Most waterfowl, with the exception of hole nesters like goldeneye, prefer not to nest where there are many trees. The other main area of vegetation management necessary to maintain good conditions for wildfowl is therefore the prevention of scrub and trees invading the waterside habitat, especially the nesting cover areas.

It is advisable that any trees planted to give shelter to the water and add variety to the habitat should be kept at least 30m away from the water's edge. Islands in particular should therefore, unless they are very large, be kept entirely free of trees. The shade under a dense, closed tree canopy will reduce the height and density of the ground cover plants which are essential for nest concealment. Trees within a nesting area also provide observation perches for crows and magpies, making their nest-finding more efficient.

Once an area has been cleared of trees and scrub the woody growth will quickly regenerate unless some form of control is exercised. Cut stumps must be treated with a suitable herbicide such as "Garlon" in diesel oil, or "Roundup" poured into notches on the stump, and any regrowth has to be sprayed with a translocated chemical such as Roundup. We have found that leaving a goat or two on an island to eat down the vegetation in late summer and through the autumn is a very effective way of preventing scrub invasion of the nesting sites. The growth of the herbaceous plants in the following spring is very strong, with a high species diversity, providing excellent conditions for nesting wildfowl.

As described in Chapter 3, the area of nest cover surrounding the water body needs to have some sort of sheltering screen and this can effectively be provided by a strip of willow or alder coppice. Both of these prefer damp soils and both respond very well to coppice management. Coppicing an area of trees around a water body enhances it enormously, providing a patchwork habitat of gradually changing structure, which is used by a great many species. It is also extremely attractive; willows in particular exhibit a wide range of leaf form and colour, and in winter the stem colour on last year's shoots is often quite remarkable, with greens, yellows, golds, reds, oranges, purples and browns predominating.

The belt of sheltering coppice should be wide enough for it to be divided into three parallel rows running around the site, so that one row may be coppiced between October and March every second year. In this way there will always be a tall strip to provide wind shelter, an intermediate height strip and a lower strip, of two year old or recently cut stools.

As well as providing an excellent screen and shelter strip, coppice managed in this way is extremely good habitat for a wide variety of flowering plants, which make use of the different degrees of shade in the different strips. It is very rich in insect life and is ideal for a great many species of passerine birds, in particular the warblers. Ducks will also nest in the dense ground cover among the recently cut stools.

The cut material can either be used as a source of fuelwood, sold for basket making (if of suitable willow varieties) or, better for conservation purposes, stacked to make a "dead hedge" between the strips of different age coppice.

Where possible the water body, and coppice strip if you have one, should be surrounded by a protective thorny hedge. Tall, wide,

136

dense hedges are very good for nesting birds and the shelter and food provided by a hedge is beneficial to many small mammals, amphibians and reptiles. A very wide range of native species may be used for hedging, including whitethorn, blackthorn, holly, barberry, beech, field maple, wild privet, hornbeam, crab apple, guelder rose, and hazel. Once established, trimming of the hedge is best done in winter to minimise disturbance to wildlife, and it is wise to leave hedge trimming to once every two or three years or to trim a different section each year. This allows the hedge plants to fruit, to the benefit of many small birds.

Management of meadows for nest cover

Wildflower meadow seed mixtures can be sown to provide excellent nest cover, as well as being attractive to butterflies, bees, many other insects and birds. If this is done, it should be a summer flower mixture and it should be planted as described in Chapter 3. After the first establishment year it should not be cut until the early autumn, and the cut material **must** be removed. If it is left *in situ* it will not only smother the flowering plants underneath it, but the continued accumulation of litter and nutrients will favour the coarser grasses, which will take over and eliminate the more desirable, flowering, broadleaved plants.

Water management for wildfowl

The depth of water is of fundamental importance in its effects on the ecology, productivity and nature of the wildlife community which develops in any aquatic ecosystem.

The facility to control water inflow and outflow is therefore extremely important for the effective management of ponds and lakes for wildlife. So, if it is at all possible, such a facility should be built into every new pond or lake including, if it is feasible, the ability to effect a complete drawdown to dry the bed out.

If you have a system whereby you can alter the water level, it becomes possible to control vegetation by seasonal changes in level. Drawdown in the summer will dry out and kill floating-leaved and submerged aquatic plants, and winter drawdown can severely weaken stands of emergent plants if their rhizomes are exposed to hard frosts. Conversely, prolonged deep flooding in spring, before the plants begin to grow, will drown emergent and invasive marginal and marsh species.

Any low profile islands can be kept fairly free of vegetation, making excellent loafing spots, by routine annual submersion for a short period each winter, followed by drying out when the water returns to normal level. For this to be effective, such loafing islands need to be very level and only just above the surface, otherwise the depth of flooding necessary will also cause too much destruction of plant cover elsewhere around the lake.

Succession of life in new waters

Within a water body the animal life undergoes a succession of changes with time, much as the plants do. Indeed, the faunal succession is related to the vegetation changes.

In newly flooded wetland systems, which are at an earlier stage of colonisation, there is a low variety of invertebrate species present, but individuals of those species are present in very large numbers. These early colonisers are animals such as the chironomid midge larvae, which are important waterfowl foods, and there is therefore more food for breeding and juvenile wildfowl in recently developed ponds and lakes, especially where they are produced by the inundation of vegetated areas of land. This drowned vegetation provides a large amount of organic detritus as food for the invertebrates soon after flooding.

As a water body ages this detritus is broken down and used up, and in a large lake with lots of open, deeper water, the production of new litter is relatively slow, thus the early blooms of a few species of invertebrate foods for wildfowl gradually disappear. As the lake

138

matures, a greater number of species colonise the water, and invertebrate predators appear, with creatures like beetle larvae, alder fly larvae, dragonfly and damselfly nymphs and leeches becoming more numerous. These feed upon the earlier inhabitants, thus reducing their numbers and lowering the ability of the lake to feed its wildfowl population.

Fish and wildfowl competition

Given more time the freshwater fish appear and there is now a great deal of evidence that these too can significantly deplete the amount of invertebrates available for wildfowl consumption, thus reducing their productivity. At the ARC Wildfowl Centre at Great Linford, Game Conservancy scientists have demonstrated that in a 17ha gravel pit lake, the numbers of midge larvae quadrupled following the removal of 6.5 tonnes of coarse fish, principally bream, roach and perch. Diet studies also showed that the bream and the perch were in fact the main predators of the important chironomid midge larvae and pupae. Roach ate snails which are important for diving ducks.

More evidence has been found which supports the view that high fish densities can reduce wildfowl breeding success. In several studies the populations of waterfowl have been found to be higher on fish-free lakes than on those with fish. Further, in most fish-free waters, duckling production is seen to be improved. Feeding efficiency of mallard ducklings has also been shown to be greater on waters without fish, particularly in the first 10 days or so of life, when they are heavily dependent upon insects.

It can be seen, then, that to increase or maintain a high level of wildfowl breeding success it is of great importance to manage the water body to promote an abundance of those species, for example chironomid midges, which are the main waterfowl foods. It is also clear that this means maintaining the system at an early stage in succession, both of vegetation and invertebrate life, with low fish densities, in effect preventing the normal deleterious successional changes that occur as the wetland ages.

Manipulation of water level

Manipulation of the water levels is the simplest way to achieve such rejuvenation of a water body. Complete drawdown for at least one full year is very effective. It exposes the lake bed to the air so that organic matter can oxidise and release its plant nutrients in a mineral form; it significantly reduces the populations of the larger predatory invertebrates; it reduces the fish numbers, particularly if the water level can be dropped rapidly immediately after the fish have spawned, so that the eggs and fry do not survive; it allows seeding of marsh and terrestrial plants, which will boost production of wildfowl foods after reflooding, and whilst drawn down will be used extensively by waders and marsh birds.

It is recommended that if the aim is to maximise waterfowl production, shallow freshwater wetlands should be rejuvenated by drying out in this way once every five to ten years.

Obviously it is a great advantage if the water area can be made into at least two separate ponds or lakes, so that they can be drawn down at different periods, one providing a reservoir of invertebrate and bird species to assist recolonization of the other after reflooding.

Water level cycles and waders

With the facility to alter water levels it is also possible to make short term fluctuations to cater for the needs of waders at particular seasons.

Observations made at The Game Conservancy Wetlands Research Unit at the ARC Wildfowl Centre have shown that passage migrant and resident waders are attracted to inland waters by visual evidence of gradually falling water levels. The number of

140

wader species and number of individual waders increased during periods of gradual drawdown of a shallow lake.

The lure appears to be the wide bank of shiny, wet mud surface between the water and the drier mud. Once the water level stabilized, the water film on this wide bank of mud dried out, leaving a sharp interface between dry mud and shallow water, and the number of wader species and individuals declined rapidly, returning again once the water level resumed its gradual fall.

Waders can obviously recognise the good feeding conditions provided by a steady fall in water level, where fresh mud and all of the food organisms it contains is constantly available. It follows from this that to attract waders such as snipe, some areas need to be provided where water can be gradually drained off a very gently sloping shoreline, over a fairly long period. Ideally this would be done to coincide with spring and autumn wader passage, say April to May and mid-July to mid-September.

At Great Linford The Game Conservancy managed a 2ha lake in the following way, which is excellent for waders and teal; it also enhances duck breeding success:

The lake is filled in early spring, surrounding the five nesting islands with water and making them secure, while the rising water refloods the lake bed and makes a good feeding site for the ducks. It is also known that waterfowl respond positively to rising water levels in spring which attract them to the site for breeding, presumably making them confident that there will be water available later in the year for brood rearing.

The water is held at the bank top all through the nesting period until a very gradual drawdown is commenced after the peak tufted duck hatch in mid-July. This gradual fall in water levels quickly attracts large numbers of wildfowl, along with the resident lapwings, redshanks, ringed and little plovers and very soon after it starts the first passage waders appear, usually green sandpipers.

Once drawdown is complete the lake remains almost empty with large areas of bare mud to oxidize and with a great deal of very shallow water available for the immigrant teal and wigeon to use, and they really do concentrate on this area.

Alternatively it is possible to reverse this cycle, with a spring draw-down to expose the lake bed, reduce fish numbers and concentrate the invertebrates in a small volume of water for feeding birds. The exposed areas will begin to develop a covering of terrestrial plants, which will decompose on reflooding, providing food for a bloom of midge larvae. Under this regime, reflooding normally takes place in late July, the aim being to provide habitat for wintering birds; again, the shallower the better – it is ideal for teal, for example, if they can stand to feed and to sleep in very shallow water.

Temporary wetlands

Apart from drawdowns in the pond or lake, water level manipulation to improve wildfowl habitats can also extend outside the normal water line.

If water can be diverted or pumped to flow on to pasture land in winter it creates superb shallow, highly attractive feeding habitat for dabbling ducks, geese and waders. It also keeps soil temperatures high and promotes earlier grass growth in spring, with benefits to the grazier and to waterfowl and waders which will nest in the meadows later in the year. This water meadow management, however, is a highly skilled art and whilst it is simple to do to benefit the wildfowl, it takes considerable experience and local knowledge to achieve the best results for agriculture at the same time. If it is done mainly to benefit wildfowl, the land should be flooded to coincide with the arrival of the main flocks of winter migrants.

Water quality

Provided the supply is regular and reliable, the water itself should require little management. It is important, though, to prevent contamination by fertilizer run-off, silage effluent, animal manure, dairy waste, etc, which will cause over-enrichment of the pond, resulting

142

in algal blooms, increased water turbidity, loss of water plants and deterioration in plant and animal species diversity.

Polluted, over-enriched waters may be recognised by their appearance. There may be a cloudy "soapy" appearance to the water, in severe cases it may smell foul and sulphurous, with bubbles of methane gas rising to the surface, there may be dead fish, massive blooms of filamentous or single-celled algae, giving the water the appearance of a green soup, or of paint-like blue-green scum on the surface, all associated with a very sparse flora and fauna.

If any water body suffers from pollution, the immediate aim must be to stop further deterioration by identifying and stopping it at source. Any excess nutrients within the pond will remain there for a very long time, unless there is a rapid flow of clean water through the pond to flush it out. If this can be arranged it helps if the bed can be stirred up during the flushing process. But beware, the "slug" of de-oxygenated silt-laden water that this produces can have disastrous effects on life in the stream below the outlet. In a water without a good flow through, the remedy is to remove the thick layer of anoxic, over-rich sediment by dredging, taking it far from any watercourse for disposal. After this the pond may be replanted to get it back to a good condition.

Artificial enrichment and liming

Water bodies can become too rich in nutrients by uncontrolled pollution but all ponds and lakes need a degree of richness to be productive biologically. Those which are natural in origin develop a richness of flora and fauna over tens of thousands of years. New, shallow waters which are made by flooding undisturbed, previously dry land are also usually very productive, with high or at least adequate nutrient levels derived from the flooded soils and plant cover (indeed, in arable farmland areas the levels of nitrates and phosphates in new waters may well be too high).

In most cases, then, the addition of fertilizers, lime or organic matter to the water is unnecessary. Although it has been shown that the productivity of nutrient-poor acidic lochs can be raised by the addition of lime or inorganic fertilizers, the effects are unpredictable and short-lived.

If the water in naturally nutrient-poor and acid through being in a peaty upland catchment it would be totally wrong to upset the delicate balance of such a fragile system by liming or fertilizing. This would simply destroy a feature which already has a high conservation value, replacing it with a water which is uncharacteristic for the area.

If there is a need to raise the pH of an acidic lowland water, for example one supplied with water from springs in some acidic sandstones, the simplest way is to place a thick layer of chalk or limestone rocks into a long run of the inflow stream just before it enters the pond or lake. This will dissolve very slowly, increasing the calcium content of the water and decreasing the acidity slightly. A pH range of 6.0–8.2 is satisfactory for most aquatic life to thrive, though there will be some variation in species composition of the communities at the extremes of pH.

Those waters which are newly made by excavation below ground level are rather different. While such waters are rapidly invaded by the highly mobile, pioneer colonist species of plant and animal, they lack the higher nutrient status and therefore have a lower species diversity and less productivity than naturally occurring and man-made surface flooded lowland water bodies.

This is particularly true of gravel pits and excavated ponds supplied solely from surface water run-off. They are basins dug into organically poor mineral deposits, usually down to a clay substrate and, being isolated from flowing surface waters, they lack the constant replenishment of nutrients (in solution and in suspension) which is a feature of stream fed waters.

Organic enrichment

In Chapter 3 we discussed altering the substrates of new water bodies by adding a variety of rock and soil types, and in lakes made

144

by excavation there is a good case for extending this treatment to include the addition of organic detritus at an early stage.

There are several ways to achieve this enrichment. Probably the best method is to leave the excavation in a fairly dry state for a period (at least one whole summer, preferably more) before flooding. This allows the bare soils to be colonised by terrestrial plants which when flooded have the same nutrient enriching, invertebrate producing effect as the flooding of undisturbed land. It would be even better to seed the future lake bed with leafy green "manure crop" species such as mustard, clover, alfalfa, lucerne, canary grass or tree lupin.

When the water is eventually allowed in (and it may need regular pumping to remain dewatered) the decaying plants give the aquatic system an enormous boost. The root mat also helps to bind the soils, thus reducing the amount of fine material in suspension in the water, and increasing water clarity, helping the rooted water plants to become established.

If it is not possible to treat the bed over a long period in this way prior to flooding, other materials may be used to achieve similar results. In a dry excavation it should be possible to spread strawy farmyard manure or dried sewage sludge (provided it is free from heavy metal contamination) on the lake bed.

Where a new lake is already filled, the problem of lack of organic detritus may be solved in a different way. Clearly what is needed is an input of a suitably natural organic detritus like that which enters the lake when the emergent plants die, break up and fall into the water in late winter and early spring.

At Great Linford a technique was developed to enrich new lakes using waste straw. The best rate of application is around 0.5kg per square metre of lake bed (5 tonnes per ha). The optimum time to add the straw is in March; the bales must be broken open, teased apart and the straw spread loosely on the water surface. Apply it from the windward shore, so that as it is thrown on the water it blows across the surface. On large areas it is necessary to fix floating pole barriers to divide the surface into sections, otherwise the entire straw mass will blow across to pile up on the lee shore.

After about 10 days the straw sinks to carpet the lake bed. The soluble nutrient salts and sugars rapidly leach out to be used by the water plants and the presence of the straw mat produces a major change in the physical structure of the lake bed environment. It provides much more cover and shelter for invertebrates, which were shown to increase tenfold after the addition of straw to our lake in March. It increases food supply, both directly as decomposing litter, and indirectly in the bacteria and fungi which begin decomposition. Initially the cover effect is the most important in increasing invertebrate numbers but eventually the straw decomposes completely and its nutrient and energy content enters the lake's cycle of production.

Also, like the root mat produced by allowing plants to grow on the bed before flooding, the carpet of straw helps to bind together the fine silty clay deposits on the lake bed, reducing their movement into suspension and keeping the water clear. The bacteria which break down the straw also remove nitrates and phosphates from solution in the water, denying them to planktonic algae. The spring algal blooms are therefore much reduced, water clarity further improved, and so rooted plants become established much sooner.

There are limitations to the use of such biologically active materials in water. They have a fairly rapid decay rate, with high levels of microbial activity, and in consequence they use up large amounts of oxygen and can thus be a potential source of over enriching pollution. This can obviously have deleterious effects on fish (especially in warm conditions) and on many sensitive invertebrates. Thus, while there is no doubt that they do have value in the enrichment of new waters, they must be used with great care. It is wiser to use only small amounts in relation to the total water volume and to delay stocking with sensitive fish, such as trout, until the initial surge of decomposition is over, say one year after the enrichment.

If fish are unimportant, as might be the case in waters devoted primarily to wildfowl production, the highly organic, low oxygen conditions produced by the addition of organic matter to shallow areas do in fact favour the production of very large numbers of the midge larvae which are so important as duckling foods. It is a good

146

practice to add such materials to very shallow scrapes, made around the main water body, to provide extra feeding sites for brood rearing and for waders.

Summary of wetland management for wildfowl

It may be appreciated from this chapter that the efficient management of a water body to maintain it in an optimum condition for wildfowl and other species involves quite a lot of work and an understanding of the biological processes occurring in a wetland.

It may be the case that with a de-intensification of agriculture, labour becomes more readily available and there may also in future be finance available to pay for such countryside management by farmers. However, where the aim of management is to create, improve or maintain good wildlife habitat, it may be possible to involve local people in the management. For example, the County Trusts for Nature Conservation may be able to help arrange seasonal management tasks.

The sort of management work described in this chapter (apart from the use of herbicides) is well within the ability of untrained personnel, provided they have adequate supervision and skilled guidance. It is therefore feasible to establish management agreements with local conservation bodies, many of whose members welcome the opportunity to undertake such conservation work in order to maintain some additional wildlife habitats within their area. In all cases, a detailed management plan should be drawn up, agreed to by the landowner and the managing body, and this must form a working document to be adhered to by both parties. Should you wish to control the management directly, the British Trust for Conservation Volunteers will provide labour and trained, experienced supervisors for conservation work at a relatively low cost.

CHAPTER NINE

Mallard Production, Incubation, Rearing and Release

Wild mallard are a native species which have a high potential for reproduction. Given good care and keepering, a shootable surplus should be obtainable on most wetland areas. There are certain situations where natural production may not offer the amount of sport required. In these circumstances it is fairly easy to rear and release some mallard to top up the wild population. There is a problem, however; mallard become tame very readily, and producing good wild birds is far from easy. Many shoots have tried this over the years and eventually given up in disgust.

For those whose aim in releasing gamebirds is not to produce sport, but to "put something back to replace those shot last season", it is perhaps salient to recognise that the wise use of a mallard population should not be detrimental anyway. In many senses it would be far better to manage and improve habitats in the ways suggested in this book and to control predation during the breeding season. This would have more lasting benefit than simply releasing a few birds.

"Creep" feeders for wild ducklings

The survival of the wild hatched ducklings can be very variable; many are no doubt lost to predators, especially mink, foxes, pike, feral cats and occasionally crows, and so local predator control is advisable throughout the rearing season. In addition, the natural food supply can be inadequate to support all of the ducklings hatched, particularly if the water contains a large population of fish. If this is so it is a good idea to provide food for the ducklings.

The best way to do this is to provide "creep feeders", which exclude the adults, which otherwise harry the ducklings and prevent them feeding. They also consume an excessive amount of the food provided for the ducklings.

It is surprising how soon wild hatched ducklings will find and use such feeding stations, and their survival as a result is usually excellent. The simplest form of "creep" consists of an old broody coop placed near the water's edge, on a fairly open grassy section of shore, with chick crumbs and grain inside them. The more such feeding stations the better, as this increases the chances of the ducklings finding them, and reduces competition. Larger feeders can be made with 5cm² weldmesh sides, which will allow ducklings in but will exclude adults (Figure 60).

The best way to use these is to build them on floating rafts, with sloping ramps for easy access. These should be moored alongside the shore until the ducklings find them and begin to feed from them, when they can then be pulled out into the open water, using a running loop around a couple of posts. In this way the feed is removed from the attention of rats and the feeding ducklings are safer out on the water than they are on shore. Initial siting of the feeder rafts

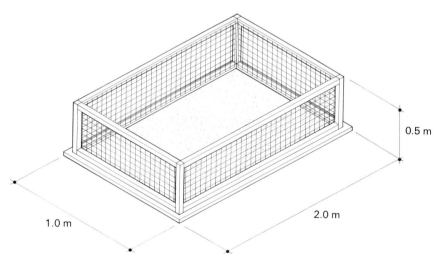

Figure 60. A "creep feeder" for ducklings with mesh sides to exclude the adult birds. (The roof netting is not shown).

149

where the adults are used to feeding will also help the ducklings
to start using them.

Picking up early eggs

If she loses her first clutch of eggs a female mallard will, provided
she has access to an abundant supply of invertebrates or other
protein-rich food, readily produce a second clutch two or three
weeks later, which she may then hatch and rear herself. This potential for production can be taken advantage of, significantly increasing the number of young produced by each female, by collecting
the early eggs to incubate them, rearing the ducklings and releasing
them when old enough.

There is a general licence issued under the terms of the Wildlife
and Countryside Act of 1981, which allows mallard eggs to be collected until the end of March in England and Wales and to April
14 in Scotland. The collected eggs *must* be incubated and every
attempt must be made to rear the ducklings. The Act also requires
that the young birds be released into the wild not later than the
end of July, and neither the eggs nor the birds may be sold or traded.

Catching-up laying birds

If you cannot rely on increasing the wild duckling survival, or on
picking up enough early mallard eggs for your requirements, they
can either be bought from game farms or produced from penned
birds caught up on your pond. This normally presents no difficulty,
providing the birds are from a "managed" strain and not truly wild.

The Game Conservancy is frequently asked to recommend a suitable catcher for waterfowl. Probably no one type is much better
than another, but the model illustrated works very successfully
(Figure 61).

It is constructed on 4cm × 2cm framing, the floor planked with
15cm × 1cm boards, and covered in 1cm mesh wire netting (except

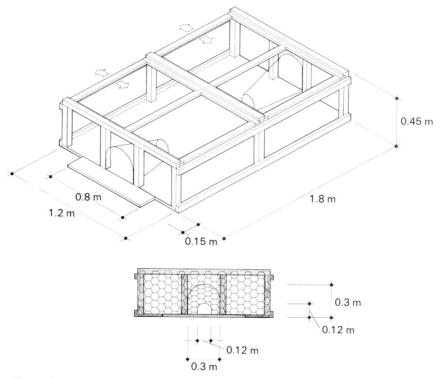

Figure 61. A floating cage trap baited with corn is an effective way to catch ducks for the laying pen.

the sliding lid, for which 4cm or 5cm mesh should be used to allow small birds to escape). The catcher is separated into two halves by a partition in order to facilitate the removal of the birds.

Using plastic containers or expanded polystyrene for buoyancy, the catcher is floated near the site where the ducks are usually fed. Normal feeding is discontinued, the trap is baited (using cut maize and barley) and the sliding lids left off. As soon as the duck are seen to be taking the bait freely (this may be after a day or so, but it can sometimes be only a matter of hours!), the catcher can be set by closing the lids. It is convenient to do this during the afternoon, removing the trapped birds early the following morning.

151

Larger "walk-in" catchers can be used, similar in size and shape to crow cages, but with funnel entrances at water level. These are best placed on a sloping beach partly in and partly out of the water, sited so that the half-submerged funnel entrance faces the shore. Diving ducks can be caught in these traps if the funnel is completely submerged – but they are also able to escape more easily!

For legal reasons the birds must be caught *before* the end of the shooting season. They should be held in a roofed laying pen, where they must be fed correctly to promote the production of good quality eggs. Caught-up mallard should be fed on mixed barley and breeders' pellets, gradually increasing the pellets until the barley is eliminated by the end of the second week of captivity. Some breeders prefer to continue scattering a little barley about (in the water, if present) to keep the drakes busy and to discourage them from harrying the females. A hopper is needed for pellets, but grain can be scattered in the open. Specially formulated wildfowl foods are now available from some feed manufacturers.

The laying pen and egg production

There is some difference of opinion regarding the ideal sex ratio in a laying pen, also the question of using immobilised birds as against free-winged, and whether deep water is necessary to enable the drakes to tread properly. We know from one game farm's experience that 100 hand-reared, wing-clipped mallard ducks penned with 10 drakes, and with only shallow drinking pans for water, can give good egg production and excellent fertility.

The system used by The Game Conservancy at Fordingbridge with caught-up stock was equally satisfactory. The laying pen was 12m², roofed with plastic netting, and enclosed a pool measuring 12m × 1.5m. Eighteen ducks and six drakes were put into this each spring and regularly produced 900–1000 eggs, with over 90% fertility. Production occurred from the first week in April to the last week in May.

A duck laying pen invariably becomes very muddy, particularly when any water is enclosed, and dirty eggs are the result. It has been found the duck will usually lay in artificial nests, if provided. Oil drums, lying on their sides with one end cut open and one-third buried, have proved satisfactory and eggs laid in straw placed inside them are cleaner.

Most eggs are laid before 9 am, and should be picked up soon after this, particularly if you have wing-clipped birds in an open-topped pen where jackdaws and crows can be troublesome.

Incubation of mallard eggs

Eggs from penned mallard should be collected daily and any visibly dirty ones cleaned gently with dry wire wool. All eggs should the be washed using a proprietary egg sanitiser following the manufacturer's instructions. The eggs should be allowed to dry before being stored blunt end up in cool, humid conditions at 10°–13°C. No turning is necessary if the eggs are stored for less than a week, but after this the egg trays should be tilted daily. It is best not to store the eggs for longer than two weeks.

A broody hen of a large variety can comfortably cover up to 15 mallard eggs, hatching taking about 26–28 days from setting. The nest boxes should be kept damp by sprinkling the eggs with tepid water from the 15th to the 24th day, and again once the first eggs chip, after which they should not be disturbed until the hatch is complete.

It is also quite possible to achieve good hatches from mallard eggs set in incubators. Those set in still-air types should be turned twice daily until the 24th day. In forced-air incubators the normal practice is for the eggs to be turned five times each day, until transference to the hatcher on the 24th day.

In very dry conditions it helps to spray the eggs very lightly with warm water from the 10th to the 23rd day, but the development of the air space should be watched carefully. If kept too damp this will be too small, resulting in many dead-in-shell chicks on the point of hatching. Candling duck eggs to watch development is quite easy. It should be done at least at the 10 day stage and again before transfer to the hatcher. Infertile, addled, or dead-in-shell eggs should be removed as they will almost certainly affect some of the adjacent eggs, reducing the hatch.

Raising mallard ducklings

Mallard are easy to rear, and it can be tempting to rear too large a number to stock the pond or lake sensibly. All that is required to attract wild birds in is about 10 ducks to an acre of pond. Overstocking with such decoys can be detrimental in a number of ways. In order to ensure that there is sufficient food available for any wild birds which flight in, so much has to be fed daily that the stocked birds become grossly overfed and too fat to fly.

Too many birds will cause serious erosion damage to the banks where they feed and scramble in and out of the water, destroying the vegetation, and their droppings not only foul the banks but also over-enrich the water, causing it to turn dark, foul and smelly, reducing its conservation value to almost nil. It is not unknown for the introduced residents to drive away any wild birds which come in to attempt to feed.

Obviously though, if the aim is to have enough birds to provide a drive on a shooting day, more birds will be needed and at least 100 will have to be reared. In considering this the limitations of your water body should be accepted. It needs at least an acre of water for this number if they are not adversely to affect it, and even then an artificially high density of ducks may reduce the general wildlife and conservation value of the area.

Once hatched, it is fairly simple to rear the ducklings. If a broody hen is used to hatch them, she and her brood should be housed in a moveable pen with a suitable coop for shelter. Incubator hatched birds need an artificial brooder inside a wire run.

154

The equipment for rearing a batch of 80–100 mallard is much the same as for 120 pheasants. An overhead heater, using electricity or bottled gas, is placed in a 1.5m² hut sited on gravel over grass. The temperature at ground level should be approximately 32°C for day-olds, and the ground should be allowed to warm up before they are introduced. The heater must be gradually raised by a few centimetres each week. The aim should be to have them weaned off heat by day at the age of three weeks, putting the heater on at night only for a further week or so, and raising it a little more each day. They can, in normal circumstances, be off heat altogether by five weeks, though in good weather they can be off in four weeks or less.

A roofed-over run measuring 9m × 3m will provide adequate space and, compared with pheasant poults, mallard ducklings will soon make the ground on which they are reared very dirty. Rearing in moveable units is therefore recommended, and ideally one should move the pen at least twice during the rearing period.

Incubator hatched mallard do not develop the waterproofing of their down as quickly as wild ducklings, and it is safer to keep them away from water of swimming depth for the first week or two. If allowed to get into the water they may become waterlogged and in bad weather they will soon become chilled and die. Adequate water for drinking and face washing must always be available and ducklings use and waste a considerable amount in a day. It is wise to keep the water supply well away from the food trays, otherwise the birds will waste large amounts of food in the drinkers.

Mallard will thrive on ordinary chick starter crumbs for the first week or ten days, but proper wildfowl crumbs are also available. Then the proportion of starter pellets (mini pellets) should be increased over the next week, gradually weaning them onto grower pellets at 3–4 weeks of age. At 6–7 weeks introduce small amounts of wheat or barley, and progressively increase the proportion of this in their food until they are receiving grain as their staple diet. By this time they should be in their release pen, normal practice being to transfer them to the release site when fully hardened off and "weather-proof" at 6–7 weeks of age.

Releasing mallard onto a pond or lake

Some form of pen on the release site is essential for you to introduce the birds to their new home. It should be of a suitable size, around 40m × 20m for 150 birds, in a sheltered position, with at least one third built to enclose the water. To keep foxes out the wire should be of 5cm mesh, 2m tall, with 20cm turned out at the top and the same amount turned out and buried or pegged down at the base. Mink are also a serious threat to penned birds, while both these and foxes can cause heavy losses in the early "post-release" phase. For this reason it is wise to have mink and fox control measures in place in the release area from the moment the birds arrive. This is discussed in greater detail in Green Guide No.7.

Once in the pen they should be fed daily, by hand, though if this is not possible one can use an automatic feeder or hoppers, in which case the ducklings should have been introduced to the same type of hoppers in their rearing unit.

At around 8–9 weeks of age they will be able to fly out of the pen, so there should be some funnel entrances to allow them to return, though many will in fact fly back in. Once the ducks are flying the feeding should continue inside the pen but the amount should gradually be reduced, while an increasing amount is fed outside the pen, encouraging them to use the whole water body. Light feeding should be continued throughout the winter, to hold the birds.

The amount of food to give requires careful judgement, based on the birds' behaviour and how quickly they consume what is given. If they become reluctant to come to the feed, they are probably being over fed. The aim should be to give just enough to keep them in good condition and to hold them on the water – too little and they will leave, too much and they will become fat and lazy!

The time and place of feeding are equally important, and the regular feeding can be used to encourage the birds to become strong flyers. Ideally the ducks should be fed both morning and evening, and it is essential to whistle or call while spreading the feed; they will soon become accustomed to this feeding signal and will fly to the feeding point. The afternoon feed should be close to the release point, but the morning feed, when reared ducks are usually most hungry, should be gradually moved further away each day. Once the birds will fly to the feeding place in response to the whistle or call you can vary the feeding place to overcome the problem of the ducks swimming to the regular feeding site and waiting around in anticipation of a feed. If they do not know where the next feed is to be they will fly to it on hearing the signal, thus developing their use of flight, making them much more of an asset on shoot days.

This system can be used even on very small ponds, putting the morning feed in a nearby field, and steadily feeding the ducks away from the release point. If possible they should be gradually led away in an uphill direction as this makes it more likely for them to fly back to the pond – they find it difficult to walk down a steep hill. If they are used to being fed each morning away from the pond this can be used on a shooting day, feeding them out in the morning as usual, then driving them back over the Guns, which should between the feed site and the pond or lake but well away from the water so they are shown high, fast, sporting shots, not birds which are simply dropping into the pond. Keeping the Guns away from the shoreline also helps to avoid a build-up of spent lead pellets in the water, thus reducing the chances of lead poisoning of your reared duck. This will, of course, be less of a problem once lead shot is phased out in wetland areas in Britain, probably in 1997.

Disease

Mallard are easily reared, but they can be subject to many of the diseases seen in gamebirds, although the course of any disease may be different. Also, life in an aquatic habitat increases the incidence of some diseases, especially those caused by many parasitic worms and the bacterial toxin disease, botulism.

As already mentioned, young ducklings grow well on balanced foods, but soon show the effects of poor quality diets, being suscep-tible to gut irritants which can produce enteritis and diarrhoea, signs similar to those of avian cholera and salmonellosis. Poor quality diets and old, stale poultry feeds are often deficient in vitamin A, which can result in a staggering gait, partial paralysis, a white or yellowish discharge from the eyes and "white eye" where the cornea becomes opaque. This vitamin deficiency also predisposes the birds to infections and parasitic disease and losses from such causes can be high. It is quite simple to avoid them by giving only good quality feed, which may be backed up with a vitamin supplement given in the drinking water.

The viral Newcastle disease (Fowl Pest) is not the killer for wildfowl that it is in gamebirds, but great care must be taken if it does occur, as mallard can be carriers. It is a legal requirement to notify the Ministry of Agriculture if it is suspected or diagnosed.

Salmonellosis, a bacterial disease, is not especially common, but if it does occur mortality in a rearing unit can be very high. Since transmission is often via the egg it is not advisable to incubate batches from a variety of sources, as an infected egg from one place could spoil a whole hatch of otherwise uncontaminated eggs. Any infected birds should be treated with furazolidone in the feed but the survivors may remain carriers of the bacterium and should not be used for breeding.

Under certain conditions, where there is warm, dirty, stagnant water, highly lethal toxins are produced by the bacterium *Clostridium botulinum*, causing many deaths. Moderate numbers of birds and clean conditions in the rearing and releasing units, with plenty of cool clean water, will prevent this occurring.

Young ducks in particular are prone to attack by an opportunistic fungus, *Aspergillus fumigatus*, which is normally found in rotting vegetation, but is able to block the windpipe and invade lungs and air sac membranes causing severe respiratory problems and death. This disease is not treatable; the aim is to prevent infection by spores carried in the air. The main source of the fungus is straw, cut grass, hay or grain, allowed to go mouldy, producing vast numbers of spores under warm, damp conditions. For this reason ducks should not be bedded on hay or straw, nor should grain feed by provided in large piles at the water's edge.

Cyathostoma, a parasitic worm similar to *Syngamus*, the gapeworm, may be found in the trachea of ducks, causing respiratory problems, but without the "gaping" signs associated with *Syngamus*. This can cause high mortalities in young ducks, and if found it may be treated with levamisole.

Young mallard often die from *Acuaria uncinata* infestations, a parasite which depends on the water flea, *Daphnia*, to maintain its complex life cycle. Although modern anthelmintics can be tried, *Acuaria* is easier to control by providing conditions where the water flea cannot maintain its numbers.

Tapeworms are commonly seen in waterfowl but rarely cause problems. Flatworms are far less common but can be more troublesome. Again both groups require secondary hosts.

The main means of keeping diseases at bay in duck rearing areas is to maintain a high degree of cleanliness and good husbandry. They must have clean, fresh water, good quality food, plenty of space, and adequate warmth, with good ventilation. Given all of these, diseases should present few problems.

If you do experience sudden or unexplained losses among reared ducklings, it is always wise to seek advice from a veterinary surgeon.

*Our Advisory Guide No.6, Diseases of Gamebirds and Wildfowl, published in 1988, covers this whole subject in greater detail and can be obtained from The Game Conservancy's Sales Centre (telephone 0425 652381).

CHAPTER TEN

Sporting Use of Ponds and Lakes

The use of a farm pond for country sports (as opposed to recreational water sports) falls into two main areas: fishing and shooting. Both of these are covered here, but as the emphasis of the book is on wildfowl, greater detail is given on shooting than on fishing.

Fishing

Providing the pond is correctly designed and managed, and stocked with good coarse fish or trout, fishing is easy to arrange. It should be noted that stocking of a water body with fish of any species is covered by Section 30 of the Salmon and Freshwater Fisheries Act, and requires the consent of the NRA Fisheries Officer. Similarly, the removal and transport of fish from a water body is subject to local Water Authority By-laws, and will require prior clearance from the Fisheries Officer which may entail a health check on the fish.

To improve the quality of the fishing it helps to clear some gaps in the reeds along the bank to give access to the water, preferably adjacent to the deeper "holes" in the pond bed. This will be where weed growth will be less and where fish tend to congregate. The banks of each swim should be reinforced with a wall of posts driven in vertically, with earth packed behind them to make a platform to fish from (Figure 62).

This idea can be developed further to provide stable fishing platforms extending a little way into the water (Figure 63).

These can limit the damage to marginal aquatic plants by confining the angler to specific sites, where they have easier access to the open water beyond the fringe of plant growth. They are particularly good where fishing facilities are provided for disabled or wheelchair-bound anglers. Many anglers now use the very long lightweight carbon fibre rods. These are very good conductors of electricity and it is therefore extremely important not to have an angling water anywhere close to overhead power cables. These are normally uninsulated and there have been numerous fatalities involving anglers whose carbon fibre rods have come close to power lines – they do not have to touch. Under quite ordinary conditions the power can arc over a considerable gap.

If the primary use of the pond is to be fishing then the shorelines should have some long peninsulas running out into the water to

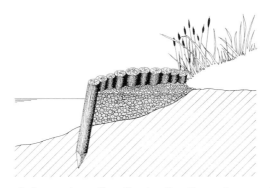

Figure 62. Regularly used angling "swims" will need some form of bank reinforcement.

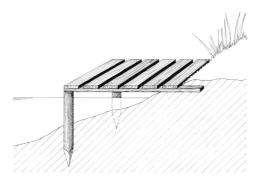

Figure 63. Fishing platforms also prevent shoreline erosion by anglers and can be used to define angling "swims".

161

extend the reach of the angler, bringing all parts of the pond within casting range. On a large enough pond, or lake, these may be 50m (60 yards) apart, allowing anglers to cover all of the water between them.

Use of a water for fish production

The presence of anglers does result in inevitable disturbance of the wildfowl and other wildlife, can cause waterfowl deaths through discarded hooks and line, increases bank erosion and damage to waterside vegetation and create traffic, access, parking and litter problems. In addition, their presence may be considered to be too intrusive in an otherwise quiet and secluded habitat.

If for any such reasons you do not wish to see your water used by anglers, but still wish to generate an income from its potential for fish, you may do so by leasing it to an angling club as a stock pond. Tench and carp are the most worthwhile species to culture. For an annual rent, they are given clearance to net and remove fish from the water on an annual or biennial basis, using the fish to re-stock other waters. Alternatively, you could arrange for the pond to be netted occasionally by a coarse fish dealer, who will then pay you for the value of the catch after deducting his netting fee and expenses.

In these times of diversification of farm enterprises, there is considerable scope for using ponds and lakes to grow fish as a crop for food or re-stocking sporting fisheries, with the added possibility of growing a harvestable crop of signal crayfish (*Pacifostacus leniusculus*) at the same time. (MAFF/NRA/EN consent is needed for stocking). **Never** stock signal crayfish in waters which communicate with native crayfish habitats, as disease (crayfish plague) may be spread to threatened wild stocks.

In intensive fish culture, the fish will need to be fed and the high stocking density will probably have adverse effects on the value of the pond as a wildfowl habitat. For this sort of operation the fish species should be chosen with due regard to the character of the

162

water. The various species of carp are probably the best for still-waters. Experience has shown that trying to rear trout at commercially viable high densities in stillwaters causes many problems with pollution, nitrogen enrichment and de-oxygenation resulting from the accumulation of their waste and uneaten food. Carp and tench are much more tolerant of such conditions.

If, however, the pond is primarily for waterfowl it is advisable not to stock heavily with bottom feeding fish such as carp or bream, which tend to churn up the pond bed, eat the wildfowl food invertebrates and destroy plant growth. Tench and Crucian carp are less destructive in this respect than carp or bream. As described in Chapter 8, a *high* density of any fish species is undesirable in a wildfowl production habitat – Game Conservancy research has shown that fish and waterfowl compete for the supply of food in the form of pond animals. Tench or Crucian carp at densities less than 100kg/ha are probably compatible with waterfowl. Perch in particular, and trout too, feed selectively on insect pupae just before and as they emerge as the adult form, which is when the ducklings find them most available. Bream have been shown to consume very large numbers of midge larvae, so it would be wise to keep perch, trout or bream populations at a low density if the main aim is the production of waterfowl. There is a ready market for all species of quality coarse fish and so the regular reduction of fish numbers and sale of the netted fish could help to pay for good management of the pond. Coarse fish for stocking angling waters generally produce a better financial return than trout, and tench are probably the most profitable species, followed by carp.

Shooting

The shooting on a farm pond or lake may take several forms. In practice every situation is a little different and the precise details of how to get the best sporting shooting from a particular water body will vary from site to site. The following notes are therefore a broad generalization on the ways in which ponds and lakes can be used to provide shooting, and if you are considering using the water body for sporting purposes it is worth seeking specialist advice. Like fish harvesting and angling, the shooting can generate a considerable income if it is correctly managed. The staff of The Game Conservancy's Advisory Service have a great deal of experience in this field and can be relied upon to give sound practical advice on the best way to capitalize on the shooting and fishing value of any water body.

Flight ponds

At its simplest and best a pond will be used for shooting wary wild duck as they flight into it at dusk to feed. To make this successful the pond needs to be kept as quiet as possible and it should have the natural food supplemented by regular daily feeds of a small amount of wheat or barley. A 10 litre bucket would be sufficient to feed 90 mallard. This should be broadcast into shallow water, preferably on a hard gravel bed, and the rate of feed should be adjusted to the number or birds using the pond. Count the birds coming into the pond as often as you can – but do not disturb them – and if food is left over in the morning, reduce the amount provided.

If the pond is large enough, covering say more than 10ha, then it may be better to shoot it at the dawn flight, as birds move to use it as a day roost after their overnight feeding on local farmland. In such cases, the feeding is not so important, though some light feeding will help to maintain the tradition of duck use of the water during the day.

Hides

However the pond is used for shooting, an adequate number of hides need to be made to allow a good choice whichever the wind direction. A well made hide must screen the Guns from the birds and

164

should serve to restrict the shooting to safe angles in respect of the other hides. Each hide should therefore face an area of open sky against which the birds may be seen, and each must have a well defined safe "arc of fire" – preferably marked by tall padded poles at the hide corners, past which a gun may not be swung. It is also a good idea to build the hide with a high back, to reduce the extent to which the Gun is silhouetted.

The usual size for a hide is 2.0m by 1.5m, with the longer side facing the water, with a minimum height of 1.5m. It is a good idea to have an extra screen available which a tall Gun can fix to the top of the hide to make it more effective. The wooden framework of the hide should be covered with panels of reeds or straw sand-wiched between two sheets of wire netting, held together by battens at the top, bottom and middle. Once a permanent site has been found for each hide, it is a good idea to plant a growing shrub screen around each one. In time these plants, such as *Lonicera nitida*, wild privet or thorn, will grow sufficiently to conceal the hide and can be clipped to the desired height. This provides the ideal straggly top edge through which the Gun can peer at approaching birds.

Unless floored, the inside of the hide will soon become a mud-bath, making it slippery and dangerous, as well as being uncomfort-able for the dogs. A slatted wooden floor, such as a couple of pallets covered with fine mesh wire netting is ideal, and even just a pad of several layers of chicken wire will help to keep the hide floor in better condition. It is also useful to build in a shelf for cartridges, torch, coffee flask, etc.

Evening flighting

Flight shooting is best arranged as a last-minute affair when strong winds provide ideal conditions. Good, steady, experienced dogs are absolutely essential – collecting "swimmers" in the dark is not easy. Guns should choose their clothing to match the environment, hide their faces by peering through the cover and, above all, *keep still*! A hat with a narrow brim which shields the face but does not force the wearer to tip his face skywards to see the duck also helps conceal the Gun. Unless you are an expert, duck calls are best not used.

The flight shooting should be infrequent, once every three weeks at the most; any more frequently and most ponds will cease to be used by the ducks. Shooting should also stop early to allow the pick-up to be completed so that the pond can be left quiet well before the end of the flight. This preserves a "lead-in" to the next flight time.

The shooting is best for everyone if the Guns shoot as a well-disciplined team. Someone is elected as "captain" – preferably someone who is not actually shooting – and this person watches the ducks in, allows them to come down almost to water level, or the first birds to land, at which point they stand up, shout and/or blow a whistle to spring the ducks and make them fly up, flaring out and away from the pond. This makes a very exciting and more testing form of shooting (especially with teal) and gives more of the Guns a chance of a shot, with the benefit of most shots being aimed up and away from the pond.

The possibility of lead poisoning

Although there is very little hard scientific evidence that lead poisoning is a major cause of large scale wildfowl mortalities in Britain, both ducks and geese do ingest spent pellets on occasion, sometimes with adverse effects. Lead shot does not decay and will accumulate around ponds where shooting takes place regularly. Over a long period this build-up can produce high levels of spent pellets, and flight ponds are therefore a potential source of lead poisoning in wildfowl, which can pick up the pellets when feeding on corn spread in the water.

The contamination of the pond by lead shot is reduced if the ducks are shot at either as they move away from the pond or, if taken as "incomers", by shooting away from the pond. The important thing is to try to avoid the spent shot falling into the water, and

166

the hides should be sited so that most of the spent shot falls on the land away from the water.

Spent lead shot is most probably eaten by ducks in mistake for grit. Certainly the incidence of ingested lead pellets has been found to be greatest among birds shot after feeding in areas where the soils are soft muds, lacking natural grits. If a flight pond has a soft bottom and muddy banks, the risk of wildfowl picking up spent lead pellets while gritting can be greatly reduced by supplying large amounts of grit to "dilute" the lead level. Crushed limestone grit is the best type to supply as it has been shown that its high calcium level helps to reduce the rate of uptake of lead salts and thus ameliorates the toxic effects of ingested lead.

Steel shot for wildfowling

Although lead poisoning from spent shot does not appear to be affecting British wildfowl populations significantly, there is now a timetable for change-over to steel (soft iron) or other non-toxic shot for wildfowling. Suitable cartridges are not yet widely available, but much progress has been made with the powder charges and shot composition of such loads. Over the first 40m of range, their ballistic performance compares favourably with that of lead, provided that a larger shot size is selected so that the striking energy of each pellet is sufficient.

Because each steel pellet is larger than a lead pellet of the same weight, and because the same number of pellets is needed to ensure an adequate full pattern of shot, the volume of the steel load is much greater. However, taking two examples, steel No.2 shot has the same striking energy and roughly the same number of pellets as the same weight of lead No.4 shot, although taking up more room in the cartridge. Similarly, steel No.4 is comparable to lead No.6 in both striking density and pattern quality **at ranges up to 40m.**

The reduced space in the cartridge necessitates a thinner wad between shot and powder if the steel load is to fit into a standard length cartridge case and this can affect the ballistic performance.

167

The combination of the less compressible wad and the harder shot means that the expanding powder gases meet a more solid charge to propel. This would increase the breech pressures unless a slower burning powder is used. This makes it difficult to produce good ballistics and it can give the impression that steel loaded cartridges have a sharper "kick".

There is a further marginal ballistical effect in that the air resistance is greater on the larger steel pellet, which slows them down a little, reducing striking energy at ranges over 40m. On the other hand, the pattern with steel shot may be better because there is no flattening of individual pellets in their passage along the barrel, as there is with lead, and so there may be less wayward "fliers" moving away from the edges of the pattern. Thus, provided a steel shot two sizes larger than the lead shot normally used is selected, the relative pattern qualities and effectiveness of lead and steel shot at 35–40m are very comparable.

Damage to gun barrel walls by steel shot has been a problem in the past, but now full length, thicker, hard plastic cup wads are incorporated into the cartridges and these protect barrel walls from abrasion. However, steel shot will not deform as it meets the constriction of the chokes in the same way that lead shot will, so it is recommended that one restricts the use of steel shot to guns which are open bored, with no greater degree of choke than improved cylinder, and at present they are not recommended for use in lightly built English or imported English-type shotguns. Most new guns, whether of English or imported origin, are built with the change-over to steel in mind.

Reports from wildfowlers in the USA who have used steel shot indicate that, once the shooter has adapted to the slightly different velocity characteristics of them (they are a little faster than lead over the first 40 metres or so), they are almost equal to lead in actual practice. The number of birds wounded rather than killed outright by steel shot as opposed to lead is according to some users slightly greater, but according to others it is slightly less. Those who have used steel shot extensively in the USA state that it is more important than ever not to attempt shots at ducks at over 35–40m range.

168

The use of reared duck

One of the best ways to use reared duck as a sporting asset is to treat the pond as a drive, standing Guns in the open well back from the pond to give the birds a chance to gain height and speed once they are driven off. Alternatively, at the end of the day's shoot, the Guns move towards the pond, put the birds off, take cover and shoot as they return.

Quality of released stock

There is a widely held view that mallard which originate from a long-domesticated stock, such as those inevitably developed by many commercial suppliers, are less willing to fly than birds from the true wild population. They may also be less good than wild birds at hatching and rearing their own young in subsequent seasons. It is therefore a great benefit to the sporting value of the water if it is made and managed so that it produces successful broods of wild duck each year.

Where domesticated mallard are regularly released the local population soon becomes dominated by them, with a reduction in their value as sporting birds. In this situation the introduction of a higher proportion of wild mallard genes into the local stock is of great benefit. This can be achieved by selective shooting of all of the drake mallard at the end of the season in late January. Such is the drive of the wild mallard drake to find a mate that the culled birds will soon be replaced by drakes from the local wild population, thus producing wilder, more flighty progeny from the resident females.

The conservation value of flight ponds

Although designed to allow the taking of a harvest from the wild duck population, flight ponds are probably not detrimental to the wildfowl population as a whole. Winter mortality in mallard appears to be density dependent, so that if the autumn and winter population is reduced by shooting, the lower density means that mortality due to other causes will be less, thus the population can compensate for the shooting mortality (provided it accounts for less than 36% of the autumn population – above this level shooting mortality appears to be additive to other causes of death, and can reduce the size of the breeding population in the following year). Also, many of the birds using such ponds will benefit from the extra food provided and will survive the shooting, thus enabling them to return to their breeding grounds in good condition. The use of a pond for wildfowl shooting is likely to take place on only 10-12 occasions per year, between September and January, and if properly designed and well managed the pond itself provides good habitat for wildfowl and other wetland species in the remaining 350 or so days of the year when it is in not shot over.

APPENDIX 1

Sources of information and further reading

Wildlife after Gravel. The Game Conservancy 1992.

The restoration of gravel pits for wildfowl. Michael Street, Published by ARC Ltd, The Ridge, Chipping Sodbury, Bristol, Avon.

Waterways and wetlands. Pub. in 1981 by the British Trust for Conservation Volunteers, 36 St Mary's Street, Wallingford, Oxford, OX10 0HL.

Ducks, ponds and people. John Swift, published by the British Association for Shooting and Conservation, Marford Mill, Rossett, Wrexham, Clwyd.

Design, construction and maintenance of earth dams and excavated ponds. E F Granfield. Pub. in 1971 by the Forestry Commission, Forest Record No. 75.

Guidelines for the use of herbicides on weeds in or near watercourses and lakes. Published by MAFF as booklet No. B2078, from MAFF Publications, Lion House, Alnwick, Northumberland, NE66 2PF.

Aquatic weed control. Chris Seagrave. Pub. in 1988 by Fishing News Books Ltd, 1 Long Garden Walk, Farnham, Surrey.

Pesticides: Guide to the new controls. MAFF leaflet No. UL79. Pub. 1987.

British waterplants. S M Haslam, C S Sinker & P A Wolseley. Pub. in 1975 by the Field Studies Council, 62 Wilson Street, London EC2A 2BU.

A guide to identifying British aquatic species. Pub. 1982 by Nature Conservancy Council.

The Crayfish, its nature and nurture. Roy E Groves. Pub. 1985 by Fishing News Books Ltd, Farnham.

APPENDIX 2

Useful Addresses

The ARC Wildfowl Centre, Wolverton Road, Great Linford, Milton Keynes, Bucks, MK14 5AH

The Arboricultural Association, Brokerswood House, Brokerswood, Westbury, Wiltshire, BA13 4EH

Aquatic Weed Research Unit, c/o Department of Applied Zoology, University of Reading, Whiteknights, Reading, Berkshire.

British Trust for Conservation Volunteers, 36 St Mary's Street, Wallingford, Oxford, OX10 0HL

British Association for Shooting and Conservation, Marford Mill, Rossett, Wrexham, Clwyd, LL12 0HL

Butyl rubber pond liners: Butyl Products Ltd., Radford Crescent, Billericay, Essex.

Ciba Geigy Agrochemicals, Whittlesford, Cambridge, CB2 4QT

The Countryside Commission, John Dower House, Crescent Place, Cheltenham, Gloucester, GL50 3RA

The Countryside Commission for Scotland, Battleby, Redgorton, Perth, PH1 3EW

The Countryside Council for Wales, Plas Penrhos, Fford Penrhos, Bangor, Gwynedd, LL57 2LQ

English Nature, Northminster House, Peterborough, PE1 1UA

Farming and Wildlife Advisory Group, The Lodge, Sandy, Beds, SG19 2DL

The Game Conservancy, Fordingbridge, Hampshire, SP6 1EF

ICI Agrochemical, Woolmead House, Bear Lane, Farnham, Surrey, GU9 7UB

The Institute of Fisheries Management, Secretary, 22 Rushworth Avenue, West Bridgford, Nottingham, NG2 7LF

The Institute of Freshwater Ecology (formerly The Freshwater Biological Association), The Ferry House, Far Sawrey, Ambleside, Windermere, Cumbria, LA22 0LP

Joint Nature Conservation Committee, Northminster House, Peterborough, PE1 1UA

May and Baker Ltd, Romford Road, Dagenham, Essex, RM10 7XS

Monsanto PLC, Agricultural Division, Thames Tower, Burleys Way, Leicester, LE1 3TP

National Rivers Authority
Head Office
Eastbury House, 30–34 Albert Embankment, London, SE1 7TL
The Aztec Centre, Aztec West, Almondsbury, Bristol, BS12 4TD
Anglian Region
Kingfisher House, Goldhay Way, Orton Goldhay, Peterborough, PE2 0ZR
Northumbrian Region
Eldon House, Regent Centre, Gosforth, Newcastle-On-Tyne, NE3 3UD

174

North West Region
P.O. Box 12, Richard Fairclough House, Knutsford Road, Warrington, WA4 1HG
Severn Trent Region
Sapphire East, Streetsbrook Road, Solihull, West Midlands, B91 1QT
Southern Region
Guildbourne House, Chatsworth Road, Worthing, West Sussex, BN11 1LD
South West Region
Manley House, Kestrel Way, Exeter, EX2 7LQ
Thames Region
3rd Floor, Kings Meadow House, Kings Meadow Road, Reading, RG1 8DQ
Yorkshire Region
21 Park Square South, Leeds, LS1 2QG
Welsh Region
Rivers House, St. Mellons Business Park, St. Mellons, Cardiff, CF3 0LT
Wessex Region
Rivers House, East Quay, Bridgewater, TA6 4YS
Avon & Dorset Area Office, Rivers House, Sunrise Business Park, Higher Shaftesbury Road, Blandford Forum, Dorset, DT11 8ST

Polythene pond liners: Visqueen Products, Farm Road, Stockton-on-Tees, Cleveland, TS18 3RD

PVC pond liners: Transatlantic Plastics, 23 Brighton Road, Surbiton, Surrey

Royal Society for the Protection of Birds, The Lodge, Sandy, Beds, SG19 2DL

Royal Society for Nature Conservation (RSNC), The Green, Nettleham, Lincoln, LN2 2NR

Scottish Natural Heritage, 2 Anderson Place, Edinburgh, EH6 5HP

Sportsman
Game Feeds

A complete range of high quality pheasant and partridge feeds

Formulated and manufactured to the highest quality standards these feeds contain a high plane of protein nutrition for the early stages of growth in order to produce sturdy, well-feathered birds resistant to disease and chilling. Sportsman Game Feeds are available nationwide and are fully supported by nutritional advice and after sales service.

Slimbridge
Wildfowl Feeds

A comprehensive range of feeds ... suitable for all types of waterfowl, and formulated to meet the requirements of The Wildfowl Trust at Slimbridge.

Particular attention has been paid to the nutritional demands of waterfowl to ensure high fertility and hatchability during the breeding season, followed by strong growth and good feathering of young birds without excessive weight gain.

WILDLIFE AFTER GRAVEL

by Nick Giles

Twenty Years of Practical Research by
The Game Conservancy and ARC

The issue of mineral extraction can be an emotive one. The dilemma between the need for essential building materials, and the fear of destroying wildlife habitats to obtain them, poses a long-term problem. At the same time there is the important question of what to do with mineral sites once they are exhausted.

The Game Conservancy Trust, funded by ARC, conducted research for twenty years on a worked-out gravel pit in Buckinghamshire. We evolved a successful strategy of management to restore the pit and create a valuable wildfowl haven. The ARC Wildfowl Centre near Milton Keynes is now a nationally significant wildlife reserve.

Wildlife After Gravel leads you from the initial development of the lakes, through the various problems encountered on the way, to management plans for the 1990s and beyond. Illustrated throughout in colour, *Wildlife After Gravel* provides vital evidence that mineral extraction does not necessarily herald the end of conservation.

Wildlife After Gravel (134pp., hardbacked) costs £19.45 (incl. postage & packing). To order your copy, telephone 0425 652381, or write to The Game Conservancy, Fordingbridge, Hants, SP6 1EF.

THE GAME CONSERVANCY

'Conservation through wise use'